AFFORDABLE
EATS

TASTE OF HOME BOOKS • RDA ENTHUSIAST BRANDS, LLC • MILWAUKEE, WI

Taste of Home

**INTERNATIONAL STANDARD BOOK
NUMBER:** 978-1-61765-790-0
**LIBRARY OF CONGRESS CONTROL
NUMBER:** 2018951858

DEPUTY EDITOR: Mark Hagen
SENIOR ART DIRECTOR: Raeann Thompson
EDITOR: Amy Glander
SENIOR DESIGNER: Courtney Lovetere
DESIGNER: Arielle Jardine
COPY EDITOR: Amy Rabideau Silvers

PHOTOGRAPHER: Jim Wieland
MARKET PRODUCER/SET STYLIST:
Stacey Genaw
SENIOR FOOD STYLIST: Shannon Roum
PICTURED ON FRONT COVER:
So-Easy Sloppy Joes, p. 87; Seasoned Fries,
p. 150

PICTURED ON TITLE PAGE:
Skillet Mac & Cheese, p. 139

PICTURED ON BACK COVER:
Pulled Pork Grilled Cheese, p. 180; Sheet-Pan
Pineapple Chicken Fajitas, p. 27; Garlic Lemon
Shrimp, p. 128; Root Beer Float Pie, p. 240

Printed in China
1 3 5 7 9 10 8 6 4 2

CONTENTS

GET SOCIAL WITH US

LIKE US: facebook.com/tasteofhome | **PIN US:** pinterest.com/taste_of_home

FOLLOW US: @tasteofhome | **TWEET US:** twitter.com/tasteofhome

TO FIND A RECIPE:
tasteofhome.com

TO SUBMIT A RECIPE:
tasteofhome.com/submit

TO FIND OUT ABOUT OTHER
TASTE OF HOME **PRODUCTS:**
shoptasteofhome.com

START SAVING MONEY TODAY!

Cut down your grocery bill, beat the clock and surprise your family with the comforting favorites they crave. It's a snap with the 113 easy, economical and enticing recipes inside **Taste of Home Affordable Eats.**

From dinner classics and weeknight wonders to impressive desserts, hearty sandwiches, hot soups and swift snacks, these mouthwatering dishes keep flavor at premium without taking bites out your budget.

Consider entrees such as Chicken Cordon Bleu Skillet (p. 15), Lemon Pork with Mushrooms (p. 35), Sheet-Pan Pineapple Chicken Fajitas (p. 27) or Grilled Brats with Sriracha Mayo (p. 23). These meals ring up at $10 or less!

You'll even find breakfast and lunch ideas that don't break the bank, as well as economical appetizers, side dishes and homemade jam, sauces and condiments. Save money and savor sensational foods today. It's easy with **Affordable Eats** at your fingertips!

SAVE TIME, TOO!

Look for these icons when you need dinner fast—while keeping money in your wallet.

◆ **FAST FIX** These sensational recipes come together in 30 minutes or less.

▶ **5 INGREDIENTS** With the exception of water, salt, pepper, oil and optional ingredients, these dishes call for only a handful of items.

● **SLOW COOKER** Come out ahead when you let your slow cooker do the work.

BIG SAVINGS START WITH A LITTLE PLANNING

Become a smarter, savvier shopper when you brush up on these easy ideas for slashing your grocery bills.

Start by creating a weekly or monthly food budget. Allocating a certain amount of money for food expenses instantly sets you up for success because you're more likely to seek out sales and less likely to make impulse purchases.

Once your budget is set, plan to shop no more than once per week. After all, the fewer times you shop, the more you'll save—on time and gas, as well as money. Visiting the store once a week also gets you into the cost-saving habit of planning meals for a week, versus ordering pizza, hitting a drive-thru or returning to the store for additional groceries.

Before shopping, take inventory of your fridge, freezer and pantry. Make a shopping list of what you need and take note of what you don't. When you're at the store, you won't impulse-buy an item you already have, and you won't be wondering about what else you might need. Once your grocery list is made, clip any applicable coupons. Be sure to use coupons only for the items on your shopping list.

In fact, make coupons your new best friends. Pick up a copy of the Sunday paper each week and start clipping, or hit the internet and take advantage of online coupons. Don't forget to make the most of your grocer's weekly specials and membership programs.

When it's time to head for the store, make sure you have your shopping list, coupons and a full stomach. You've heard it before but it bears repeating: Don't go grocery shopping on an empty stomach. The temptation to buy things that aren't on your list can be too great for any hungry shopper to avoid.

FINE-TUNE YOUR SHOPPING STRATEGIES

Once you're ready to shop, keep these tips in mind.

BUY IN BULK. Consider membership with a warehouse or food club. Buying food and supplies in larger quantities can dramatically cut costs in the long run. Stock up on items such as rice, canned goods and other pantry staples, and watch for specials on family-favorite meats you can freeze.

PAY ATTENTION TO WEIGHT. There's no better place to be concerned about weight than at the grocery store. An item's sticker price can only tell you so much, but look a little closer and you'll see how much it costs per ounce or gram. Compare different brands, and different amounts between brands, to score the best deal.

KNOW A SALE WHEN YOU SEE IT. Think twice when a sale sign catches your attention. If something's on sale, but your family doesn't need it, then it's not a sale for you. If you can't enjoy the food before it goes bad, that's not a sale for you, either. And two items packaged together at a "special price" isn't a sale if you can buy those items separately for less.

BUY GENERIC. Store brands are usually cheaper than name brands—even when you have a coupon for the name brand. Always compare prices and consider buying generic. Concerned about flavor or quality? Buy just one item and see if you like it before making it a mainstay.

VISIT THE INTERNATIONAL AISLE. Surprise! You often can find better deals on rice, spices, canned goods, tortillas, beans and other staples in the ethnic aisle than in other areas of the supermarket.

BE A LOYAL SHOPPER. Variety may be the spice of life, but it isn't the best way to save money when you're buying groceries. Frequenting one store will help you learn about its promotions, such as double-coupon days. And be sure to sign up for the loyalty program. You'll rack up rewards, get the inside scoop on markdowns and possibly score some freebies.

BID THE CASHIER ADIEU. Opt for the self-checkout line. The wait time is generally shorter, and you'll have less chance to linger around sweets and the other last-minute temptations near the cashier. You'll also be more conscious of what you're buying, which will give you the opportunity to reconsider any impulse items that might have wandered into your cart.

LOOK FOR SUBSTITUTES. Saving isn't about cutting out what makes you happy but about shopping smarter. Each time you get back from the store, review your receipts to find the most expensive items. Can you substitute something else, or a less expensive brand, next week?

GROCERY SHOPPING GUIDELINES—AISLE BY AISLE

PRODUCE SECTION

- Buy fresh fruit and vegetables only when on sale and when in season.

- Beware of "buy one, get one free" offers on produce. It's a good deal only if you can use the produce before it spoils.

- Before buying bags of apples, oranges, onions or potatoes, make sure none of the items are bruised or spoiled.

- Instead of purchasing expensive bagged salad greens, buy them whole instead. Whole vegetables tend to last a bit longer, and you get more bang for your buck in the long run.

MEATS & SEAFOOD

- It's more economical to buy meats in whole (such as pork roasts, large beef cuts, a package of ground beef and whole chickens) than it is to buy "convenient" cuts (like steak for stir-fry dishes, hamburger patties, pork chops and boneless skinless chicken breasts).

- Look for inexpensive beef cuts and tenderize them by marinating or slow-cooking.

- Walk past cuts of meat that have already been marinated, stuffed or seasoned, because they will generally be more expensive. Do the seasoning at home.

- Try other sources of protein, such as canned tuna, salmon and beans.

FROZEN FOODS

- Turn to frozen fruits and vegetables when fresh varieties are not in season and are more expensive.

- Don't buy veggies with sauces. They're more expensive (and not as good for you, either).

- Skip buying frozen pancakes, French toast and waffles and make your own. Freeze leftovers for fast breakfasts in the future.

CREATE A COST-EFFECTIVE PANTRY

Have you ever bought a duplicate item because you couldn't remember if you already had one at home? Have you ever picked up a can from your shelves only to see that the expiration date has come and gone? Do you continue to buy canned goods even though you already have plenty to use?

It's time to stop needlessly overstocking your pantry by getting organized. These tips can help.

1. Empty everything out of the pantry and put it on a counter or table.

2. Wipe down the pantry shelves and dry thoroughly.

3. Decide to save or discard each item. If you know that you'll never use an unopened item (and if it's not past the expiration date), donate it to a local food pantry.

4. Group like items together:
- Baking items (mixes, frosting, decorating items)
- Beverages and drink mixes
- Canned fruits and vegetables
- Canned soups
- Cereals and breakfast items
- Paper goods like plates and napkins
- Pasta and rice
- Sauces and condiments
- Snacks

5. Restock your shelves, keeping the following in mind:
- Place heavy items like soda and juice bottles on bottom shelves.
- Turn items so you can easily read labels.
- Place frequently used items at eye level.
- Label shelves so the family can put the items away in the correct spots.
- Rotate items as you restock so the first in is the first out.

6. Make two lists as you work: one for items to add to your grocery list and one for an inventory of items in the pantry. Mount the inventory list inside the pantry along with a pen or pencil. Update as you use or add items.

7. Clean out the pantry every six months.

DAIRY
- Need shredded cheese? Buy a block and shred it at home. You'll be surprised at the flavor and cost savings.

- Check the milk prices at your local gas station mini mart. Milk is often less expensive there than in the supermarket.

BREADS, CEREALS & PASTA
- Give day-old breads a try. They're cheaper and are perfect for toast, bread crumbs and stuffing.

- Bulk hot cereals cost less than the individual packets.

- Bigger boxes of cold cereal are more economical than individual boxes.

- Plain pasta and rice are more affordable than kits or mixes with sauces.

MEALS FOR $10

These budget-friendly meals will feed your family without busting your wallet. Not including basic pantry staples you already have in your arsenal, each dish comes to about $10!

THAI COCONUT BEEF

My husband and I love Thai food, but going out on weeknights can be challenging with our busy schedules. I created this Thai-inspired dinner that can double as a quick and easy lunch for the next day. The beef in this recipe is fantastic, but chicken or pork would be equally good.
—Ashley Lecker, Green Bay, WI

PREP: 30 min. • **COOK:** 7¾ hours • **MAKES:** 10 servings

- 1 boneless beef chuck roast (3 lbs.), halved
- 1 tsp. salt
- 1 tsp. pepper
- 1 large sweet red pepper, sliced
- 1 can (13.66 oz.) coconut milk
- ¾ cup beef stock

- ½ cup creamy peanut butter
- ¼ cup red curry paste
- 2 Tbsp. soy sauce
- 2 Tbsp. honey
- 2 tsp. minced fresh gingerroot
- ½ lb. fresh sugar snap peas, trimmed

- ¼ cup minced fresh cilantro
- Hot cooked brown or white rice
- Optional toppings: thinly sliced green onions, chopped peanuts, hot sauce and lime wedges

1. Sprinkle beef with salt and pepper. Place beef and pepper slices in a 5-qt. slow cooker. In a bowl, whisk coconut milk, beef stock, peanut butter, curry paste, soy sauce, honey and ginger; pour over meat. Cook, covered, on low 7-8 hours or until meat is tender.

2. Remove beef; cool slightly. Skim fat from reserved juices. Shred beef with two forks. Return beef to slow cooker; stir in snap peas. Cook, covered, on low 45-60 minutes longer or until peas are crisp-tender. Stir in cilantro. Serve with rice and, if desired, toppings of your choice.

FREEZE OPTION: Place cooled meat mixture in freezer containers and freeze. To use, partially thaw in the refrigerator overnight. Microwave, covered, on high in a microwave-safe dish until heated through, gently stirring and adding a little broth or water if necessary.

1 CUP: 421 cal., 28g fat (14g sat. fat), 88mg chol., 731mg sod., 12g carb. (7g sugars, 2g fiber), 32g pro.

OUR TWO CENT$
Red curry paste, a combination of Asian spices (lemongrass, lime leaves, etc.), can add an amazing flavor punch to your dishes. Look for it in the ethnic aisle of your grocery store.

CHICKEN CORDON BLEU SKILLET

Here's a speedy stovetop version of classic chicken cordon bleu. I often toss in sliced mushrooms if I have them on hand. Cooked veggies like broccoli or cauliflower are delicious additions, too.
—Sandy Harz, Spring Lake, MI

TAKES: 25 min. • **MAKES:** 4 servings

- 8 oz. uncooked medium egg noodles (about 5 cups)
- 1 lb. boneless skinless chicken breasts, cut in 1-in. pieces
- ½ tsp. pepper
- 1 Tbsp. butter
- 1 can (10¾ oz.) condensed cream of chicken soup, undiluted
- ½ cup shredded Swiss cheese
- ½ cup cubed fully cooked ham
- ¼ cup water
- Minced fresh parsley

1. Cook egg noodles according to package directions; drain.

2. Meanwhile, sprinkle chicken with pepper. In a large skillet, heat butter over medium-high heat; saute the chicken just until browned, 3-5 minutes. Stir in soup, cheese, ham and water; cook, covered, over medium heat until cheese is melted and chicken is no longer pink, 6-8 minutes, stirring occasionally. Stir in the noodles. Sprinkle with parsley.

1½ CUPS: 516 cal., 18g fat (8g sat. fat), 147mg chol., 878mg sod., 47g carb. (2g sugars, 3g fiber), 40g pro.

OUR TWO CENT$
To make cubed cooked chicken for recipes, simmer some boneless chicken breasts in a little water seasoned with salt, pepper and your favorite herbs. Cool and dice; keep the chicken pieces in the freezer to pull out when needed.

SALMON WITH HORSERADISH PISTACHIO CRUST

Impress everyone at your table with this elegant but easy salmon. Feel free to switch up the ingredients to suit your tastes. You can substitute scallions for the shallot or try almonds or pecans instead of pistachios. The nutty coating also plays well with chicken and pork.
—Linda Press Wolfe, Cross River, NY

TAKES: 30 min. • **MAKES:** 6 servings

- 6 salmon fillets (4 oz. each)
- ⅓ cup sour cream
- ⅔ cup dry bread crumbs
- ⅔ cup chopped pistachios
- 1 shallot, minced (about ½ cup)
- 2 Tbsp. olive oil
- 1 to 2 Tbsp. prepared horseradish
- 1 Tbsp. snipped fresh dill or 1 tsp. dill weed
- ½ tsp. grated lemon or orange zest
- ¼ tsp. crushed red pepper flakes
- 1 garlic clove, minced

Preheat oven to 350°. Place salmon, skin side down, in an ungreased 15x10x1-in. baking pan. Spread sour cream over each fillet. Combine remaining ingredients. Pat crumb-nut mixture onto tops of salmon fillets, pressing to help coating adhere. Bake until fish just begins to flake easily with a fork, 12-15 minutes.

1 SALMON FILLET: 376 cal., 25g fat (5g sat. fat), 60mg chol., 219mg sod., 15g carb. (3g sugars, 2g fiber), 24g pro. **DIABETIC EXCHANGES:** 3 lean meat, 2 fat.

OUR TWO CENT$

For best results, be sure to use plain horseradish, not horseradish sauce or creamed horseradish in this recipe. Try 1 Tbsp. horseradish for a nice mild flavor. For a little more bite, increase to 2 or 3 Tbsp.

PRESSURE COOKER BEEF TIPS

These beef tips remind me of a childhood favorite. I cook them with mushrooms and serve over brown rice, noodles or mashed potatoes.
—Amy Lents, Grand Forks, ND

PREP: 20 min. • **COOK:** 15 min. • **MAKES:** 4 servings

- 3 tsp. olive oil
- 1 beef top sirloin steak (1 lb.), cubed
- ½ tsp. salt
- ¼ tsp. pepper
- ⅓ cup dry red wine or beef broth
- ½ lb. sliced baby portobello mushrooms
- 1 small onion, halved and sliced
- 2 cups beef broth
- 1 Tbsp. Worcestershire sauce
- 3 to 4 Tbsp. cornstarch
- ¼ cup cold water
- Hot cooked mashed potatoes

1. Select saute setting on a 6-qt. electric pressure cooker and adjust for high heat. Add 2 tsp. oil. Sprinkle beef with salt and pepper. Brown meat in batches, adding oil as needed. Transfer meat to a bowl. Add wine to cooker, stirring to loosen browned bits. Return beef to cooker; add the mushrooms, onion, broth and Worcestershire sauce. Lock lid; make sure vent is closed. Select manual setting; adjust pressure to high and set time for 15 minutes. When finished cooking, quickly release pressure according to the manufacturer's directions.

2. Select saute setting and adjust for high heat; bring liquid to a boil. In a small bowl, mix the cornstarch and water until smooth; gradually stir into beef mixture. Cook and stir until the sauce is thickened, 1-2 minutes. Serve with mashed potatoes.

1 CUP: 212 cal., 7g fat (2g sat. fat), 46mg chol., 836mg sod., 8g carb. (2g sugars, 1g fiber), 27g pro. **DIABETIC EXCHANGES:** 3 lean meat, ½ starch, ½ fat.

OUR TWO CENT$
The next day, stir a little heavy cream or sour cream into leftover sauce and serve over pasta.

BROCCOLI-PORK STIR-FRY WITH NOODLES

I combined several recipes to come up with this one that my family declared a winner—it's everything we crave in a stir-fry. I sometimes substitute boneless, skinless chicken breasts for the pork.

—Joan Hallford, North Richland Hills, TX

TAKES: 30 min. • **MAKES:** 4 servings

- 6 oz. uncooked whole wheat linguine
- 2 Tbsp. cornstarch
- 3 Tbsp. reduced-sodium soy sauce
- 1½ cups reduced-sodium chicken broth

- 3 green onions, chopped
- 1½ tsp. canola oil
- 1 pork tenderloin (1 lb.), cut into bite-sized pieces
- 1 Tbsp. minced fresh gingerroot

- 3 garlic cloves, minced
- 1½ lbs. fresh broccoli florets (about 10 cups)
- 1 Tbsp. sesame seeds, toasted

1. Cook linguine according to package directions; drain and keep warm. Whisk cornstarch into soy sauce and broth until smooth; stir in chopped green onions.

2. In a large nonstick skillet, heat the oil over medium-high heat; stir-fry pork 3 minutes. Add ginger and garlic; cook and stir until the pork is browned, 2 minutes. Remove from pan.

3. Add broth mixture to skillet; bring to a boil. Cook and stir until thickened, 1-2 minutes. Add broccoli; reduce heat. Simmer, covered, until broccoli is crisp-tender, 5-8 minutes. Stir in pork; heat through, 2-3 minutes.

4. Serve over linguine; sprinkle with toasted sesame seeds.

1 SERVING: 376 cal., 8g fat (2g sat. fat), 64mg chol., 595mg sod., 47g carb. (4g sugars, 9g fiber), 35g pro. **DIABETIC EXCHANGES:** 3 lean meat, 2 starch, 2 vegetable, ½ fat.

OUR TWO CENT$
Try this as a cold noodle salad for lunch, but don't limit the veggies to just broccoli. Toss in carrots, snap peas, sprouts or whatever suits your taste!

GRILLED BRATS WITH SRIRACHA MAYO

I am a Sriracha fanatic, so guess what ingredient inspired this dish? You can boil the brats in your favorite beer to reduce the fat and give them flavor before grilling. Garlic butter spread on lightly toasted buns is delicious, too.
—Quincie Ball, Olympia, WA

TAKES: 20 min. • **MAKES:** 4 servings

- ½ cup mayonnaise
- ⅓ cup minced roasted sweet red peppers
- 3 Tbsp. Sriracha Asian hot chili sauce
- 1 tsp. hot pepper sauce
- 4 fully cooked bratwurst links
- 4 brat buns or hot dog buns, split
- ½ cup dill pickle relish
- ½ cup finely chopped red onion
- Ketchup, optional

Mix first four ingredients. Grill bratwursts, covered, over medium-low heat until browned and heated through, 7-10 minutes, turning occasionally. Serve in buns with mayonnaise mixture, relish, onion and, if desired, ketchup.

1 SERVING: 742 cal., 49g fat (13g sat. fat), 65mg chol., 2020mg sod., 54g carb. (10g sugars, 2g fiber), 20g pro.

HEALTH TIP: Sausage, bread and condiments all contain high levels of sodium. To cut back, skip the relish and use half of the sweet-spicy sauce. You'll save more than 600mg of sodium per serving.

VEGETARIAN PAD THAI

Here's my version of pad Thai loaded with crisp, colorful vegetables and zesty flavor. Give fresh and simple a twirl.
—Colleen Doucette, Truro, NS

TAKES: 30 min. • **MAKES:** 4 servings

- 6 oz. uncooked thick rice noodles
- 2 Tbsp. packed brown sugar
- 3 Tbsp. reduced-sodium soy sauce
- 4 tsp. rice vinegar
- 2 tsp. lime juice

- 2 tsp. olive oil
- 3 medium carrots, shredded
- 1 medium sweet red pepper, cut into thin strips
- 4 green onions, chopped
- 3 garlic cloves, minced

- 4 large eggs, lightly beaten
- 2 cups bean sprouts
- ⅓ cup chopped fresh cilantro
  Chopped peanuts, optional
  Lime wedges

1. Prepare rice noodles according to the package directions. Drain; rinse well and drain again. In a small bowl, mix together brown sugar, soy sauce, vinegar and lime juice.

2. In a large nonstick skillet, heat the oil over medium-high heat; stir-fry carrots and pepper until crisp-tender, 3-4 minutes. Add green onions and garlic; cook and stir for 2 minutes. Remove from pan.

3. Reduce heat to medium. Pour eggs into same pan; cook and stir until no liquid egg remains. Stir in the carrot mixture, noodles and sauce mixture; heat through. Add bean sprouts; toss to combine. Top with cilantro and, if desired, peanuts. Serve with lime wedges.

1¼ CUPS: 339 cal., 8g fat (2g sat. fat), 186mg chol., 701mg sod., 55g carb. (15g sugars, 4g fiber), 12g pro.

SHEET-PAN PINEAPPLE CHICKEN FAJITAS

I combined chicken and pineapple for a different flavor on our fajitas. They're more on the sweet side, but my family loved them!
—Nancy Heishman, Las Vegas, NV

PREP: 20 min. • **COOK:** 20 min. • **MAKES:** 6 servings

- 2 Tbsp. coconut oil, melted
- 3 tsp. chili powder
- 2 tsp. ground cumin
- 1 tsp. garlic powder
- ¾ tsp. kosher salt
- 1½ lbs. chicken tenderloins, halved lengthwise
- 1 large red or sweet onion, halved and sliced (about 2 cups)

- 1 large sweet red pepper, cut into ½-in. strips
- 1 large green pepper, cut into ½-in. strips
- 1 Tbsp. minced seeded jalapeno pepper
- 2 cans (8 oz. each) unsweetened pineapple tidbits, drained
- 2 Tbsp. honey

- 2 Tbsp. lime juice
- 12 corn tortillas (6 in.), warmed
  Optional toppings: pico de gallo, sour cream, shredded Mexican cheese blend and sliced avocado
  Lime wedges, optional

1. Preheat oven to 425°. In a large bowl, mix the first five ingredients; stir in chicken. Add onion, peppers, pineapple, honey and lime juice; toss to combine. Spread mixture evenly in two greased 15x10x1-in. pans.

2. Roast for 10 minutes, rotating pans halfway through cooking. Remove the pans from oven; preheat broiler.

3. Broil the chicken mixture, one pan at a time, 3-4 in. from heat until the vegetables are lightly browned and chicken is no longer pink, for 3-5 minutes. Serve in tortillas, with toppings and lime wedges as desired.

2 **FAJITAS:** 359 cal., 8g fat (4g sat. fat), 56mg chol., 372mg sod., 45g carb. (19g sugars, 6g fiber), 31g pro. **DIABETIC EXCHANGES:** 3 starch, 3 lean meat, 1 fat.

OUR TWO CENT$
If you love pineapple, add even more as a topping or serve with a fruity peach or pineapple salsa. If you don't have coconut oil on hand, substitute with canola or vegetable oil.

SMOKY SPANISH CHICKEN

After enjoying a saucy chicken dish at a Spanish tapas restaurant, my husband and I were eager to make our own version at home. The crispy chicken skin is tasty, but if you want to cut the fat, just remove it after browning.

—Ryan Haley, San Diego, CA

TAKES: 30 min. • **MAKES:** 4 servings

3 tsp. smoked paprika
½ tsp. salt
¼ tsp. pepper
1 Tbsp. water

4 bone-in chicken thighs
1½ cups baby portobello mushrooms, quartered
1 cup chopped green onions, divided

1 can (14½ oz.) fire-roasted diced tomatoes, undrained

1. Mix first four ingredients; rub over chicken.

2. Place a large skillet over medium heat. Add chicken, skin side down. Cook until browned, 4-5 minutes per side; remove from pan. Remove all but 1 Tbsp. drippings from pan.

3. In drippings, saute mushrooms and ½ cup green onions over medium heat until tender, 1-2 minutes. Stir in tomatoes. Add chicken; bring to a boil. Reduce the heat; simmer, covered, until a thermometer inserted in chicken reads 170°, 10-12 minutes. Top with remaining green onions.

1 SERVING: 272 cal., 15g fat (4g sat. fat), 81mg chol., 646mg sod., 10g carb. (4g sugars, 2g fiber), 25g pro.

OUR TWO CENT$
Complement the zesty, bold flavors in this chicken entree with a side of seasoned rice or sauteed bell peppers.

CHILI-LIME MUSHROOM TACOS

I used to make these tacos with ground beef, but one day decided to swap the beef for portobello mushrooms. Now we have a favorite meatless dish to add to our dinner rotation. The tacos are quick, nutritious, low fat and tasty.
—Greg Fontenot, The Woodlands, TX

TAKES: 25 min. • **MAKES:** 4 servings

- 4 large portobello mushrooms (about ¾ lb.)
- 1 Tbsp. olive oil
- 1 medium sweet red pepper, cut into strips
- 1 medium onion, halved and thinly sliced
- 2 garlic cloves, minced
- 1½ tsp. chili powder
- ½ tsp. salt
- ½ tsp. ground cumin
- ¼ tsp. crushed red pepper flakes
- 1 tsp. grated lime zest
- 2 Tbsp. lime juice
- 8 corn tortillas (6 in.), warmed
- 1 cup shredded pepper jack cheese

1. Remove stems from mushrooms; if desired, remove gills using a spoon. Cut the mushrooms into ½-in. slices.

2. In a large skillet, heat oil over medium-high heat; saute mushrooms, red pepper and onion until mushrooms are tender, 5-7 minutes. Stir in garlic, seasonings, lime zest and juice; cook and stir 1 minute. Serve in tortillas; top with cheese.

2 TACOS: 300 cal., 14g fat (6g sat. fat), 30mg chol., 524mg sod., 33g carb. (5g sugars, 6g fiber), 13g pro. **DIABETIC EXCHANGES:** 2 vegetable, 1½ starch, 1 medium-fat meat, ½ fat.

HEALTH TIP: Making these tacos with lean ground beef adds almost 4g of saturated fat per serving. That's a good reason for a meatless Taco Tuesday!

STOVETOP CHEESEBURGER PASTA

Cheeseburgers are mouthwatering in any incarnation, but I'm partial to this creamy pasta dish that tastes just like the real thing. It's weeknight comfort in a bowl.
—Tracy Avis, Peterborough, ON

TAKES: 30 min. • **MAKES:** 8 servings

- 1 pkg. (16 oz.) penne pasta
- 1 lb. ground beef
- ¼ cup butter, cubed
- ½ cup all-purpose flour
- 2 cups 2% milk
- 1¼ cups beef broth
- 1 Tbsp. Worcestershire sauce
- 3 tsp. ground mustard
- 2 cans (14½ oz. each) diced tomatoes, drained
- 4 green onions, chopped
- 3 cups shredded Colby-Monterey Jack cheese, divided
- ⅔ cup grated Parmesan cheese, divided

1. Cook penne pasta according to package directions; drain.

2. Meanwhile, in a Dutch oven, cook and crumble beef over medium heat until no longer pink, 5-7 minutes. Remove from pan with a slotted spoon; pour off drippings.

3. In same pan, melt butter over low heat; stir in flour until smooth. Cook and stir until lightly browned, 2-3 minutes (do not burn). Gradually whisk in milk, broth, Worcestershire sauce and mustard. Bring to a boil, stirring constantly; cook and stir until thickened, 1-2 minutes. Stir in diced tomatoes; return to a boil. Reduce heat; simmer, covered, 5 minutes.

4. Stir in green onions, pasta and beef; heat through. Stir in half of the cheeses until melted. Sprinkle with remaining cheese; remove from heat. Let stand, covered, until melted.

1½ CUPS: 616 cals, 29g fat (17g sat. fat), 98mg chol., 727mg sod., 56g carb. (7g sugars, 3g fiber), 33g pro.

MY TWO CENT$

"This recipe is definitely a great one to feed a big family. Both of my kids loved it because it has such a friendly, mild and familiar flavor profile for two cheeseburger-loving kids."
—SHANNONDOBOS, TASTEOFHOME.COM

LEMON PORK WITH MUSHROOMS

This is my family's favorite dish. A little squeeze of lemon gives these crispy, seasoned chops a citrusy boost.
—Christine Datian, Las Vegas, NV

TAKES: 30 min. • **MAKES:** 4 servings

1 large egg, lightly beaten	¼ tsp. salt	2 garlic cloves, minced
1 cup seasoned bread crumbs	⅛ tsp. pepper	2 tsp. grated lemon zest
8 boneless thin pork loin chops (2 oz. each)	1 Tbsp. olive oil	1 Tbsp. lemon juice
	1 Tbsp. butter	Lemon wedges, optional
	½ lb. sliced fresh mushrooms	

1. Place the egg and bread crumbs in separate shallow bowls. Sprinkle pork chops with salt and pepper; dip in egg, then coat with crumbs, pressing to adhere.

2. In a large skillet, heat oil over medium heat. In batches, cook pork chops until golden brown, about 2-3 minutes per side. Remove from pan; keep warm.

3. Wipe pan clean. In skillet, heat the butter over medium heat; saute the mushrooms until tender, 2-3 minutes. Stir in garlic, lemon zest and lemon juice; cook and stir 1 minute. Serve over pork. If desired, serve with lemon wedges.

1 SERVING: 331 cal., 15g fat (5g sat. fat), 109mg chol., 601mg sod., 19g carb. (2g sugars, 1g fiber), 28g pro. **DIABETIC EXCHANGES:** 3 lean meat, 1½ fat, 1 starch.

SPAGHETTI & MEATBALL SKILLET SUPPER

I developed this one-skillet spaghetti and meatball dish to cut down cooking time on busy nights. The beans, artichokes and tomatoes bump up the nutrition factor, while the lemon and parsley make it pop with brightness.
—Roxanne Chan, Albany, CA

TAKES: 30 min. • **MAKES:** 6 servings

- 12 oz. frozen fully cooked Italian turkey meatballs
- 1 Tbsp. olive oil
- 1 can (28 oz.) whole tomatoes, undrained, broken up
- 1 can (15 oz.) cannellini beans, rinsed and drained
- 1 can (14 oz.) water-packed quartered artichoke hearts, drained
- ½ tsp. Italian seasoning
- 1 can (14½ oz.) reduced-sodium chicken broth
- 4 oz. uncooked spaghetti, broken into 2-in. pieces (about 1⅓ cups)
- ¼ cup chopped fresh parsley
- 1 Tbsp. lemon juice
  Grated Parmesan cheese

1. Prepare meatballs according to the package directions. In a large skillet, heat oil over medium heat; add meatballs and cook until browned slightly, turning occasionally.

2. Add tomatoes, beans, artichoke hearts, Italian seasoning and broth; bring to a boil. Stir in the spaghetti; return to a boil. Reduce heat; simmer, covered, until spaghetti is tender, 10-12 minutes, stirring occasionally.

3. Stir in parsley and lemon juice. Serve with Parmesan cheese.

1⅓ CUPS: 330 cal., 10g fat (2g sat. fat), 43mg chol., 1051mg sod., 38g carb. (5g sugars, 6g fiber), 20g pro.

OUR TWO CENT$

Crushed tomatoes are a major component in the sauce in this recipe, so don't be afraid to splurge on high-quality ones. We recommend San Marzano canned tomatoes. If your kids are squeamish about tomatoes, switch to two 14-oz. cans of diced tomatoes so the pieces are smaller.

STUFFED SPAGHETTI SQUASH

I've been working on creating healthy recipes that taste tempting and keep me satisfied. This squash tossed with beef, beans and kale has so much flavor, it's easy to forget it's good for you!
—Charlotte Cravins, Opelousas, LA

TAKES: 30 min. • **MAKES:** 4 servings

- 1 medium spaghetti squash
- 1 cup water
- ¾ lb. lean ground beef (90% lean)
- ½ cup chopped red onion
- 2 Tbsp. yellow mustard
- 2 to 3 tsp. Louisiana-style hot sauce
- 4 small garlic cloves, minced
- 1 can (15 oz.) no-salt-added black beans, rinsed and drained
- 2 cups chopped fresh kale
- ¼ cup plain Greek yogurt

1. Trim ends of squash and halve lengthwise; discard seeds. Place squash, cut side down, on the trivet in a 6-qt. electric pressure cooker. Add water to cooker. Lock lid; make sure the vent is closed. Select steam setting; adjust pressure to high and set time for 7 minutes. When squash is finished cooking, quickly release pressure according to the manufacturer's directions. Set squash aside; remove water from cooker. In a large skillet, crumble beef and cook with onion over medium heat until no longer pink, 4-6 minutes; drain. Add mustard, hot sauce and garlic; cook 1 minute more. Stir in black beans and kale; cook just until kale wilts, 2-3 minutes.

2. Using a fork, separate strands of spaghetti squash; combine with meat mixture. Dollop servings with Greek yogurt.

1½ CUPS: 401 cal., 12g fat (4g sat. fat), 57mg chol., 314mg sod., 51g carb. (2g sugars, 13g fiber), 26g pro.

BREAKFAST ON A BUDGET

A hearty and comforting breakfast doesn't have to break the bank. Look here for classic sunrise specialties that use affordable, everyday ingredients. Some even call for five or fewer to keep prep easy as you hustle out the door.

SPICED PUMPKIN WARM-UP

Pumpkin spice lovers, you just met your new morning pick-me-up. Add coffee if you want an extra kick. I've also chilled this mixture and blended it with vanilla ice cream to make pumpkin shakes.
—Andrea Heyart, Aubrey, TX

TAKES: 10 min. • **MAKES:** 2 servings

2   cups half-and-half cream
3   Tbsp. sugar
2   Tbsp. canned pumpkin

1   tsp. pumpkin pie spice
¼   tsp. vanilla extract

Whipped cream
and additional pumpkin
pie spice

In a small saucepan, combine cream, sugar, canned pumpkin and pumpkin pie spice; cook and stir over medium heat until blended and heated through. Remove from heat; stir in the vanilla. Top servings with whipped cream and additional pie spice.

1 CUP: 402 cal., 24g fat (16g sat. fat), 120mg chol., 121mg sod., 28g carb. (27g sugars, 1g fiber), 8g pro.

OUR TWO CENT$
No pumpkin pie spice in the house? Make your own! Combine 4 tsp. ground cinnamon, 2 tsp. ground ginger, 1 tsp. ground cloves and ½ tsp. ground nutmeg. Store in an airtight container. Substitute for store-bought pumpkin pie spice in any recipe. Yield: 7½ tsp.

BERRY-TOPPED PUFF PANCAKE

Impressive to see and even better to taste, this gorgeous pancake is surprisingly simple to make. Add a scoop of vanilla ice cream to make it extra indulgent.

—Marie Cosenza, Cortlandt Manor, NY

PREP: 20 min. • **BAKE:** 15 min. • **MAKES:** 4 servings

- 2 Tbsp. butter
- 2 large eggs
- ½ cup 2% milk
- ½ cup all-purpose flour
- 2 Tbsp. sugar
- ¼ tsp. salt

TOPPING
- ⅓ cup sugar
- 1 Tbsp. cornstarch
- ½ cup orange juice
- 2 tsp. orange liqueur
- 1 cup sliced fresh strawberries

- 1 cup fresh blueberries
- 1 cup fresh raspberries
  Confectioners' sugar, optional

1. Place butter in a 9-in. pie plate. Place in a 425° oven for 4-5 minutes or until melted. Meanwhile, in a large bowl, whisk eggs and milk. In another bowl, combine the flour, sugar and salt. Whisk into egg mixture until blended. Pour into the prepared pie plate. Bake for 14-16 minutes or until sides are crisp and golden brown.

2. Meanwhile, in a small saucepan, combine sugar and cornstarch. Gradually stir in orange juice and liqueur. Bring to a boil over medium heat, stirring constantly. Cook and stir 1-2 minutes longer or until thickened. Remove from the heat.

3. Spoon berries over pancake, and drizzle with sauce. Dust with confectioners' sugar if desired.

1 SLICE: 320 cal., 9g fat (5g sat. fat), 123mg chol., 239mg sod., 54g carb. (35g sugars, 4g fiber), 7g pro.

HERB BREAKFAST FRITTATA

I came up with this recipe on a snowy day, using what I had in the fridge. Yukon Gold potatoes give this frittata a comforting bottom crust.
—Katherine Hansen, Brunswick, ME

TAKES: 30 min. • **MAKES:** 4 servings

- ¼ cup thinly sliced red onion
- 1 Tbsp. olive oil
- 1 large Yukon Gold potato, peeled and thinly sliced
- 6 large eggs
- 1 tsp. minced fresh rosemary or ¼ tsp. dried rosemary, crushed
- 1 tsp. minced fresh thyme or ¼ tsp. dried thyme
- ¼ tsp. salt
- ⅛ tsp. crushed red pepper flakes
- ⅛ tsp. pepper
- 2 Tbsp. shredded cheddar cheese

1. In an 8-in. ovenproof skillet, saute onion in oil until tender. Using a slotted spoon, remove onion and keep warm. Arrange potato in a single layer over bottom of pan.

2. In a small bowl, whisk the eggs, seasonings and onion; pour over potatoes. Cover and cook for 4-6 minutes or until nearly set.

3. Uncover skillet. Broil 3-4 in. from the heat for 2-3 minutes or until eggs are completely set. Sprinkle with cheese. Let stand for 5 minutes. Cut into wedges.

1 WEDGE: 204 cal., 12g fat (4g sat. fat), 321mg chol., 277mg sod., 13g carb. (2g sugars, 1g fiber), 11g pro. **DIABETIC EXCHANGES:** 1 starch, 1 medium-fat meat, 1 fat.

CHICKEN & WAFFLES

My first experience with chicken and waffles sent my taste buds into orbit. I first made the dish into appetizers, but we all love them as a main course for breakfast or dinner, too.

—Lisa Renshaw, Kansas City, MO

TAKES: 25 min. • **MAKES:** 4 servings

12 frozen crispy chicken strips (about 18 oz.)

½ cup honey
2 tsp. hot pepper sauce

8 frozen waffles, toasted

1. Bake chicken strips according to the package directions. Meanwhile, in a small bowl, mix honey and pepper sauce.

2. Cut chicken into bite-sized pieces; serve on waffles. Drizzle with honey mixture.

1 SERVING: 643 cal., 22g fat (3g sat. fat), 32mg chol., 958mg sod., 93g carb. (39g sugars, 6g fiber), 21g pro.

MY TWO CENT$

"Our granddaughter made this for supper tonight. Oh, my gosh! The complexity in something so simple! Wow! The honey-hot sauce really set it apart from the rest."

—ASNUNEZ, TASTEOFHOME.COM

DROP BISCUITS & GRAVY

We enjoy these flaky biscuits covered with creamy gravy for breakfast, yes, but also for dinner. Priced at less than a dollar per serving, it's hard to find a more stick-to-the-ribs meal at such a low price.
—Darlene Brenden, Salem, OR

TAKES: 20 min. • **MAKES:** 4 servings

- 1 cup all-purpose flour
- 1½ tsp. baking powder
- ⅛ tsp. salt
- ½ cup 2% milk

- 2 Tbsp. butter, melted

GRAVY
- ½ lb. bulk pork sausage
- 1 Tbsp. butter

- 3 Tbsp. all-purpose flour
- 1¾ cups 2% milk
- ⅛ tsp. salt
- ½ tsp. pepper

1. Preheat oven to 450°. Whisk together flour, baking powder and salt. In another bowl, whisk together milk and butter; stir into dry ingredients just until dough is blended. Drop four biscuits onto a parchment paper-lined baking sheet; bake until golden brown, 10-12 minutes

2. In a small saucepan, cook and crumble sausage over medium heat until no longer pink, for 4-5 minutes. Stir in butter until melted; sprinkle with flour. Gradually stir in milk, salt and pepper. Bring to a boil, stirring constantly; cook and stir about 2 minutes. Serve over biscuits.

1 BISCUIT WITH ⅓ CUP GRAVY: 454 cal., 27g fat (12g sat. fat), 72mg chol., 864mg sod., 36g carb. (7g sugars, 1g fiber), 16g pro.

OUR TWO CENT$
Biscuits are done when they're golden brown on the top and bottom. The sides will always be a little light. Remove to wire racks. Biscuits are best served warm, fresh from the oven.

BRATWURST HASH

The next time you make brats for dinner, save a few to toss in this quick skillet hash the next day. Making the most of leftovers saves money and is a fun way to reinvent your favorite flavors into something new.
—Marie Parker, Milwaukee, WI

TAKES: 30 min. • **MAKES:** 4 servings

- 4 uncooked bratwurst links, casings removed
- 1 medium green pepper, chopped
- 1 pkg. (20 oz.) refrigerated diced potatoes with onion
- 1 cup fresh or frozen corn, thawed
- ¼ cup chopped roasted sweet red pepper
- ¼ tsp. salt or ½ tsp. seasoned salt
- ¾ cup shredded Colby-Monterey Jack cheese

1. In a large nonstick skillet, cook bratwurst and green pepper over medium heat 4-6 minutes or just until sausage is no longer pink, breaking up sausage into large crumbles.

2. Stir in potatoes, corn, red pepper and salt; spread evenly onto bottom of skillet. Cook for 10 minutes without stirring. Turn mixture over; cook 7-8 minutes longer or until potatoes are tender. Sprinkle with cheese.

1½ CUPS: 506 cal., 31g fat (13g sat. fat), 82mg chol., 1458mg sod., 35g carb. (3g sugars, 3g fiber), 19g pro.

BAKED FRENCH TOAST WITH BLUEBERRY SAUCE

My recipe for French toast baked in the oven makes easy work of a breakfast classic. Top slices with this fruity blueberry sauce to make any day feel extraordinary.
—Debbie Johnson, Centertown, MO

PREP: 20 min. • **BAKE:** 20 min. • **MAKES:** 4 servings (1 cup sauce)

¼ cup butter, melted
4 large eggs
1 cup 2% milk
1 tsp. vanilla extract
½ tsp. ground nutmeg

8 slices Texas toast
BLUEBERRY SAUCE
¼ cup sugar
1½ tsp. cornstarch
¼ tsp. ground cinnamon

⅛ tsp. ground cloves
1½ cups fresh or frozen blueberries
2 Tbsp. thawed orange juice concentrate

1. Pour melted butter on a 15x10x1-in. baking pan; lift and tilt pan to coat bottom evenly. In a large shallow bowl, whisk the eggs, milk, vanilla and nutmeg. Dip both sides of Texas toast into egg mixture; place on prepared pan. Bake at 375° for 20-25 minutes or until lightly browned.

2. For sauce, in a large saucepan, combine the sugar, cornstarch, cinnamon and cloves. Stir in blueberries and orange juice concentrate. Bring to a boil; cook and stir for 2 minutes or until thickened. Serve with French toast.

2 SLICES FRENCH TOAST WITH ¼ CUP SAUCE: 481 cal., 20g fat (10g sat. fat), 225mg chol., 549mg sod., 63g carb. (27g sugars, 3g fiber), 14g pro.

OUR TWO CENT$
Make your French toast even richer by using flavored nondairy creamer instead of the milk in the egg-milk mixture. French vanilla creamer is especially tasty.

CRANBERRY ORANGE PANCAKES

These fluffy pancakes studded with bright red cranberries are brimming with sweet, tart and tangy flavors. Top them with melted butter and the cranberry-orange syrup to make them even more decadent. They're scrumptious for special occasions—including Christmas morning—but don't let that stop you from enjoying them all year long.
—Nancy Zimmerman, Cape May Court House, NJ

PREP: 20 min. • **COOK:** 5 min./batch • **MAKES:** 12 pancakes (1¼ cups syrup)

SYRUP
- 1 cup fresh or frozen cranberries
- ⅔ cup orange juice
- ½ cup sugar
- 3 Tbsp. maple syrup

PANCAKES
- 2 cups biscuit/baking mix
- 2 Tbsp. sugar
- 2 tsp. baking powder
- 2 large eggs
- 1 large egg yolk
- 1 cup evaporated milk
- 2 Tbsp. orange juice
- 1 tsp. grated orange zest
- ½ cup chopped fresh or frozen cranberries
  Orange zest strips, optional

1. In a small saucepan, bring the cranberries, orange juice and sugar to a boil. Reduce heat; simmer, uncovered, for 5 minutes. Cool slightly. With a slotted spoon, remove ¼ cup cranberries; set aside.

2. In a blender, process cranberry mixture until smooth. Transfer to a small bowl; stir in maple syrup and reserved cranberries. Keep warm.

3. In a large bowl, combine the biscuit mix, sugar and baking powder. In another bowl, whisk the eggs, egg yolk, milk, orange juice and zest. Stir into dry ingredients just until blended. Fold in chopped cranberries.

4. Drop batter by ¼ cupfuls onto a greased hot griddle; turn when bubbles form on top. Cook until second side is golden brown. Serve with syrup. Garnish with orange zest strips if desired.

3 EACH: 574 cal., 17g fat (7g sat. fat), 177mg chol., 1055mg sod., 94g carb. (53g sugars, 3g fiber), 12g pro.

APPETIZERS FOR LESS

Cooks who like to entertain know that food, drinks and supplies add up fast. These savory noshes and extra-special finger foods prove that it's possible to pull out all the stops without going broke. Let's get this party started!

DILL VEGETABLE DIP

A friend gave me this zesty dip recipe many years ago, and now I serve it at our annual holiday open house. To make individual servings, spoon a serving of the dip in the bottom of a clear glass cup, then garnish with fresh veggies.
—Karen Gardiner, Eutaw, AL

PREP: 5 min. + chilling • **MAKES:** 1½ cups

1 cup sour cream	1 Tbsp. finely chopped onion	1 tsp. seasoned salt
½ cup mayonnaise	2 tsp. dried parsley flakes	Assorted fresh vegetables
	1 tsp. dill weed	

Combine the first six ingredients; mix well. Cover and refrigerate. Serve with vegetables.

2 TBSP.: 107 cal., 11g fat (3g sat. fat), 17mg chol., 187mg sod., 1g carb. (1g sugars, 0 fiber), 1g pro.

OUR TWO CENT$

Dill is available as fresh leaves, dried and crushed, or seeds. It has a fresh, sweet, grassy flavor. Dill complements sour cream, cream cheese, cottage cheese, dips and spreads, meats, vegetables, eggs and potato salad.

ALMOND-BACON CHEESE CROSTINI

Try these baked bites for a change from the usual toasted tomato appetizer. For a pretty presentation, slice the baguette at an angle instead of making a straight cut.
—Leondre Hermann, Stuart, FL

PREP: 30 min. • **BAKE:** 15 min. • **MAKES:** 3 dozen

- 1 French bread baguette (1 lb.), cut into 36 slices
- 2 cups shredded Monterey Jack cheese
- ⅔ cup mayonnaise
- ½ cup sliced almonds, toasted
- 6 bacon strips, cooked and crumbled
- 1 green onion, chopped
  Dash salt
  Additional toasted almonds, optional

1. Place bread slices on an ungreased baking sheet. Bake at 400° for 8-9 minutes or until lightly browned.

2. Meanwhile, in a large bowl, combine cheese, mayonnaise, almonds, bacon, onion and salt. Spread over bread. Bake for 7-8 minutes or until cheese is melted. Sprinkle with additional almonds if desired. Serve warm.

1 PIECE: 120 cal., 8g fat (2g sat. fat), 8mg chol., 160mg sod., 10g carb. (0 sugars, 1g fiber), 3g pro.

MY TWO CENT$

"Love this recipe! Found it while going through my grandmother's Taste of Home *magazine a few years ago. It's a huge hit at holiday parties. You must make a lot because they go quickly!"*
—SMB1996, TASTEOFHOME.COM

SAVORY POTATO SKINS

Put together a plate of these crisp potato skins for a simple hot snack on your party buffet.
—Andrea Holcomb, Torrington, CT

PREP: 1¼ hours • **BROIL:** 5 min. • **MAKES:** 32 appetizers

4 large baking potatoes (about 12 oz. each)	1 tsp. salt	1 tsp. paprika
3 Tbsp. butter, melted	1 tsp. garlic powder	Sour cream and chives, optional

1. Preheat oven to 375°. Scrub potatoes; pierce several times with a fork. Place on a greased baking sheet; bake until tender, 1-1¼ hours. Cool slightly.

2. Cut each potato lengthwise in half. Scoop out pulp, leaving ¼-in.-thick shells (save the pulp for another use).

3. Cut each half shell lengthwise into quarters; return to baking sheet. Brush insides with butter. Mix seasonings; sprinkle over butter.

4. Broil 4-5 in. from heat until golden brown, 5-8 minutes. If desired, mix sour cream and chives and serve with potato skins.

1 PIECE: 56 cal., 2g fat (1g sat. fat), 6mg chol., 168mg sod., 8g carb. (0 sugars, 1g fiber), 1g pro.

SWEET POTATO-CRUSTED CHICKEN NUGGETS

I was looking for ways to spice up traditional chicken nuggets and came up with this recipe. The chips add a crunchy texture and flavor while the meat cooks up tender on the inside.
—Kristina Segarra, Yonkers, NY

TAKES: 30 min. • **MAKES:** 4 servings

Oil for deep-fat frying
1 cup sweet potato chips
¼ cup all-purpose flour

1 tsp. salt, divided
½ tsp. coarsely ground pepper
¼ tsp. baking powder

1 Tbsp. cornstarch
1 lb. chicken tenderloins, cut into 1½-in. pieces

1. In an electric skillet or deep fryer, heat oil to 350°. Place chips, flour, ½ tsp. salt, pepper and baking powder in a food processor; pulse until ground. Transfer to a shallow dish.

2. Mix cornstarch and remaining salt; toss with chicken. Toss with potato chip mixture, pressing gently to coat.

3. Fry nuggets, a few at a time, until golden brown, 2-3 minutes. Drain on paper towels.

1 SERVING: 308 cal., 17g fat (1g sat. fat), 56mg chol., 690mg sod., 12g carb. (1g sugars, 1g fiber), 28g pro.

SPICY EDAMAME

Every party needs a few tempting finger foods. Skip same-old bagged chips and pretzels and instead offer guests edamame seasoned with salt, ginger, garlic and red pepper flakes.
—*Taste of Home* Test Kitchen

TAKES: 20 min. • **MAKES:** 6 servings

1 pkg. (16 oz.) frozen edamame pods
2 tsp. kosher salt
¾ tsp. ground ginger
½ tsp. garlic powder
¼ tsp. crushed red pepper flakes

Place edamame in a large saucepan and cover with water. Bring to a boil. Cover and cook for 4-5 minutes or until tender; drain. Transfer to a large bowl. Add the seasonings; toss to coat.

1 SERVING: 52 cal., 2g fat (0 sat. fat), 0 chol., 642mg sod., 5g carb. (1g sugars, 2g fiber), 4g pro.

OUR TWO CENT$
Popular in Asian cuisine, edamame are soybeans in their pods that are harvested early, before the beans become hard. The young beans are parboiled and frozen to retain their freshness and can be found in the freezer of grocery and health food stores. Edamame is a tasty addition to soups, salads, sandwiches and main dishes or eaten alone as a healthy snack.

BROCCOLI & CHIVE-STUFFED MINI PEPPERS

Crunchy peppers perfectly balance the creamy filling in these party appetizers. Fresh chives make them stand out.
—Jean McKenzie, Vancouver, WA

TAKES: 30 min. • **MAKES:** 2 dozen

- 12 miniature sweet peppers
- 1 pkg. (8 oz.) cream cheese, softened
- 1/3 cup minced fresh chives
- 1/8 tsp. salt
- 1/8 tsp. pepper
- 2/3 cup finely chopped fresh broccoli
- 2/3 cup shredded cheddar cheese

1. Preheat oven to 400°. Cut peppers lengthwise in half; remove seeds. In a bowl, mix the cream cheese, chives, salt and pepper; stir in broccoli. Spoon into pepper halves.

2. Place on a foil-lined baking sheet; bake 9-11 minutes or until heated through. Sprinkle with cheddar cheese. Bake 3-4 minutes longer or until cheese is melted. Cool slightly before serving.

1 STUFFED PEPPER HALF: 48 cal., 4g fat (2g sat. fat), 14mg chol., 68mg sod., 1g carb. (1g sugars, 0 fiber), 1g pro.

MINI PHYLLO TACOS

Crispy phyllo cups are the secret to creating an appetizer with all the flavor and appeal of a taco—and all the fun of pop-in-your-mouth finger food. The two-bite treats of spicy ground beef and zesty shredded cheese will get a thumbs-up.
—Roseann Weston, Philipsburg, PA

PREP: 30 min. • **BAKE:** 10 min. • **MAKES:** 2½ dozen

- 1 lb. lean ground beef (90% lean)
- ½ cup finely chopped onion
- 1 envelope taco seasoning
- ¾ cup water
- 1¼ cups shredded Mexican cheese blend, divided
- 2 pkg. (1.9 oz. each) frozen miniature phyllo tart shells

1. Preheat oven to 350°. In a small skillet, cook beef and onion over medium heat until meat is no longer pink; drain. Stir in the taco seasoning and water. Bring to a boil. Reduce heat; simmer, uncovered, 5 minutes. Remove from heat; stir in ½ cup cheese blend.

2. Place tart shells in an ungreased 15x10x1-in. baking pan. Fill with taco mixture.

3. Bake 6 minutes. Sprinkle tacos with remaining cheese blend; bake 2-3 minutes longer or until cheese is melted.

FREEZE OPTION: Freeze cooled taco cups in a freezer container, separating the layers with waxed paper. To use, reheat on a baking sheet in a preheated 350° oven until crisp and heated through.

1 SERVING: 63 cal., 3g fat (1g sat. fat), 11mg chol., 156mg sod., 4g carb. (0 sugars, 0 fiber), 4g pro.

MY TWO CENT$

"Made these with kids recently and it was a big hit! Garnished mine with diced cilantro. Served alongside salsa and guacamole."
—HOMEMADEWITHLOVE, TASTEOFHOME.COM

SWEET GINGERED CHICKEN WINGS

Whenever I prepare these wings for a get-together, they're one of the first items to disappear. I first tasted them many years ago when I attended a class on using honey in cooking. Now I sometimes serve these sweetly spicy wings as a main course.
—Debbie Dougal, Roseville, CA

PREP: 10 min. • **BAKE:** 1 hour • **MAKES:** 2 dozen

1 cup all-purpose flour
2 tsp. salt
2 tsp. paprika
¼ tsp. pepper
24 chicken wings
(about 5 lbs.)

SAUCE
¼ cup honey
¼ cup thawed orange
juice concentrate

½ tsp. ground ginger
Minced fresh
parsley, optional

1. Preheat oven to 350°. Line two baking sheets with foil; coat with cooking spray.

2. In a swallow dish, combine flour, salt, paprika and pepper. Add chicken wings, a few at a time; toss to coat. Divide wings between prepared pans. Bake 30 minutes.

3. In a small bowl, combine honey, orange juice concentrate and ginger; brush over chicken wings. Bake 25-30 minutes or until the chicken juices run clear.

4. Preheat broiler. Broil wings 4 in. from heat 1-2 minutes or until lightly browned. If desired, sprinkle with parsley.

1 CHICKEN WING: 134 cal., 7g fat (2g sat. fat), 29mg chol., 225mg sod., 8g carb. (4g sugars, 0 fiber), 10g pro.

KICKIN' CAULIFLOWER

Not a fan of cauliflower? Prepare to be amazed. These crunchy bites make a smokin' appetizer that's both delish and healthy!
—Emily Tyra, Traverse City, MI

TAKES: 25 min. • **MAKES:** 8 servings

1 medium head cauliflower (about 2¼ lbs.), cut into florets

1 Tbsp. canola oil

½ cup Buffalo wing sauce
   Blue cheese salad dressing

1. Preheat oven to 400°. Toss the cauliflower with oil; spread in a 15x10x1-in. pan. Roast until tender and lightly browned, 20-25 minutes, stirring once.

2. Transfer to a bowl; toss with Buffalo wing sauce. Serve with dressing.

⅓ CUP: 39 cal., 2g fat (0 sat. fat), 0 chol., 474mg sod., 5g carb. (2g sugars, 2g fiber), 2g pro.

OUR TWO CENT$
When purchasing fresh cauliflower, look for a head with compact florets that are free from yellow or brown spots. The leaves should be crisp and green, not withered or discolored. Tightly wrap an unwashed head of cauliflower and refrigerate for up to 5 days. Before using, wash and remove the leaves at the base and trim the stem.

Affordable Entrees:
BEEF, CHICKEN & TURKEY

It's possible to satisfy the meat lover in everybody without busting your budget. Enjoy these meaty and economical recipes that call for the most popular and versatile cuts of meat—beef, chicken and turkey.

CHEESY BOW TIE CHICKEN

Here's a simple dish that tastes like it's straight from your favorite Italian restaurant. Look for spinach-artichoke dip in your supermarket's deli. It's also available frozen, just make sure to thaw it according to the package directions before prepping this recipe.
—Sally Sibthorpe, Shelby Township, MI

TAKES: 30 min. • **MAKES:** 4 servings

2 pkg. (8 oz. each) frozen spinach and artichoke cheese dip
3 cups uncooked bow tie pasta

3 cups cubed rotisserie chicken
1 cup chopped roasted sweet red peppers

⅓ cup pitted Greek olives, halved
½ tsp. salt
¼ tsp. pepper

1. Heat cheese dip according to the package directions. Meanwhile, in a Dutch oven, cook pasta according to package directions; drain, reserving ½ cup pasta water. Return to pan.

2. Stir in chicken, cheese dip, peppers, olives, salt and pepper, adding enough reserved pasta water to achieve a creamy consistency; heat through.

1½ CUPS: 453 cal., 12g fat (3g sat. fat), 93mg chol., 795mg sod., 44g carb. (4g sugars, 2g fiber), 38g pro.

FAVORITE BAKED SPAGHETTI

This yummy spaghetti casserole will be requested again and again for potlucks and family gatherings. It's especially popular with my grandchildren, who go crazy for all the ooey-gooey, melty cheese.
—Louise Miller, Westminster, MD

PREP: 25 min. • **BAKE:** 1 hour • **MAKES:** 10 servings

1 pkg. (16 oz.) spaghetti	½ tsp. seasoned salt	2 cups 4% cottage cheese
1 lb. ground beef	2 large eggs	4 cups part-skim shredded
1 medium onion, chopped	⅓ cup grated Parmesan	mozzarella cheese
1 jar (24 oz.) meatless spaghetti sauce	cheese	
	5 Tbsp. butter, melted	

1. Cook spaghetti according to the package directions. Meanwhile, in a large skillet, cook beef and onion over medium heat until meat is no longer pink; drain. Stir in spaghetti sauce and seasoned salt; set aside.

2. In a large bowl, whisk the eggs, Parmesan cheese and butter. Drain spaghetti; add to egg mixture and toss to coat.

3. Place half of the spaghetti mixture in a greased 3-qt. baking dish. Top with half of the cottage cheese, meat sauce and mozzarella cheese. Repeat layers.

4. Cover and bake at 350° for 40 minutes. Uncover; bake 20-25 minutes longer or until cheese is melted.

1¼ CUPS: 526 cal., 24g fat (13g sat. fat), 127mg chol., 881mg sod., 45g carb. (9g sugars, 3g fiber), 31g pro.

OUR TWO CENT$

We recommend using small-curd cottage cheese in this recipe because it blends in beautifully with the other ingredients. Ricotta is an excellent substitute for a milder flavor and a finer texture. If you like your casserole a bit saucier, just add a little extra sauce, or keep the casserole covered throughout baking.

EFFORTLESS ALFREDO PIZZA

Here's a light, scrumptious twist for pizza night. The recipe makes good use of leftovers and convenience items, so you don't have to spend much time in the kitchen. I often use collard greens instead of spinach.
—Brittney House, Lockport, IL

TAKES: 20 min. • **MAKES:** 6 slices

- 1 pkg. (10 oz.) frozen chopped spinach, thawed and squeezed dry
- 1 cup shredded cooked turkey breast
- 2 tsp. lemon juice
- ¼ tsp. salt
- ¼ tsp. pepper
- 1 prebaked 12-in. pizza crust
- 1 garlic clove, peeled and halved
- ½ cup reduced-fat Alfredo sauce
- ¾ cup shredded fontina cheese
- ½ tsp. crushed red pepper flakes

1. Preheat oven to 450°. In a large bowl, mix the first five ingredients until blended.

2. Place crust on an ungreased 12-in. pizza pan; rub with cut sides of garlic. Discard garlic. Spread Alfredo sauce over the crust. Top with spinach mixture, cheese and pepper flakes. Bake for 8-12 minutes or until crust is lightly browned.

1 SLICE: 302 cal., 10g fat (4g sat. fat), 45mg chol., 756mg sod., 33g carb. (1g sugars, 1g fiber), 20g pro. **DIABETIC EXCHANGES:** 2 starch, 2 lean meat, ½ fat.

SO-EASY SLOPPY JOES

Everybody in the family will love the zesty, fun flavor of this simple staple. Try it spooned over warmed corn bread instead of buns for a fun change of pace.
—Karen Anderson, Cuyahoga Falls, OH

TAKES: 30 min. • **MAKES:** 6 servings

1½ lbs. ground beef
1 can (10 oz.) diced tomatoes and green chilies, undrained
1 can (6 oz.) tomato paste

¼ cup ketchup
2 Tbsp. brown sugar
1 Tbsp. spicy brown mustard

¼ tsp. salt
6 sandwich buns, split
Fresh arugula

In a large skillet, cook beef over medium heat until no longer pink; drain. Stir in the tomatoes, tomato paste, ketchup, brown sugar, mustard and salt. Bring to a boil. Reduce heat; simmer, uncovered, for 5 minutes. Serve on buns. Top meat with arugula.

FREEZE OPTION: Freeze cooled meat mixture in freezer containers. To use, partially thaw in the refrigerator overnight. Heat the meat mixture through in a saucepan, stirring occasionally and adding a little water if necessary. Serve on buns with arugula.

1 SERVING: 478 cal., 18g fat (6g sat. fat), 70mg chol., 918mg sod., 49g carb. (15g sugars, 2g fiber), 30g pro.

CASSOULET FOR TODAY

French cassoulet is traditionally cooked for hours, but this version offers the same homey taste in less time. It's easy on the wallet, too.

—Virginia Anthony, Jacksonville, FL

PREP: 45 min. • **BAKE:** 50 min. • **MAKES:** 6 servings

- 6 boneless skinless chicken thighs (about 1½ lbs.)
- ¼ tsp. salt
- ¼ tsp. coarsely ground pepper
- 3 tsp. olive oil, divided
- 1 large onion, chopped
- 1 garlic clove, minced
- ½ cup white wine or chicken broth

- 1 can (14½ oz.) diced tomatoes, drained
- 1 bay leaf
- 1 tsp. minced fresh rosemary or ¼ tsp. dried rosemary, crushed
- 1 tsp. minced fresh thyme or ¼ tsp. dried thyme
- 2 cans (15 oz. each) cannellini beans, rinsed and drained

- ¼ lb. smoked turkey kielbasa, chopped
- 3 bacon strips, cooked and crumbled

TOPPING
- ½ cup soft whole wheat bread crumbs
- ¼ cup minced fresh parsley
- 1 garlic clove, minced

1. Preheat oven to 325°. Sprinkle chicken with salt and pepper. In a broiler-safe Dutch oven, heat 2 tsp. oil over medium heat; brown chicken on both sides. Remove from pan.

2. In same pan, saute onion in remaining oil over medium heat until crisp-tender. Add garlic; cook 1 minute. Add wine; bring to a boil, stirring to loosen browned bits from pan. Add tomatoes, herbs and chicken; return to a boil.

3. Transfer to oven; bake, covered, 30 minutes. Stir in beans and kielbasa; bake, covered, until chicken is tender, 20-25 minutes.

4. Remove from oven; preheat broiler. Discard bay leaf; stir in bacon. Toss bread crumbs with parsley and garlic; sprinkle over top. Place in oven so surface of cassoulet is 4-5 in. from heat; broil until crumbs are golden brown, 2-3 minutes.

NOTE: To make soft bread crumbs, tear bread into pieces and place in a food processor or blender. Cover and pulse until crumbs form. One slice of bread yields ½ to ¾ cup crumbs.

NOTE: Adding pulses such as cannellini beans to a meat-based main dish bumps up the fiber and protein without adding saturated fats.

1 SERVING: 394 cal., 14g fat (4g sat. fat), 91mg chol., 736mg sod., 29g carb. (4g sugars, 8g fiber), 33g pro. **DIABETIC EXCHANGES:** 4 lean meat, 2 starch, ½ fat.

CHICKEN OLÉ FOIL SUPPER

These Mexi-style chicken packets can be assembled ahead and frozen if you like. Just thaw them overnight in the fridge, then grill as directed. I like to serve them with warm tortillas and fresh fruit on the side.
—Mary Peck, Salina, KS

TAKES: 30 min. • **MAKES:** 4 servings

- 1 can (15 oz.) black beans, rinsed and drained
- 2 cups fresh or frozen corn (about 10 oz.), thawed
- 1 cup salsa
- 4 boneless skinless chicken breast halves (4 oz. each)
- ¼ tsp. garlic powder
- ¼ tsp. pepper
- ⅛ tsp. salt
- 1 cup shredded cheddar cheese
- 2 green onions, chopped

1. Mix beans, corn and salsa; divide among four 18x12-in. pieces of heavy-duty foil. Top with chicken. Mix seasonings; sprinkle over chicken. Fold foil over chicken, sealing tightly.

2. Grill packets, covered, over medium heat until a thermometer inserted in chicken reads 165°, 15-20 minutes. Open foil carefully to allow steam to escape. Sprinkle with cheddar cheese and green onions.

1 SERVING: 405 cal., 13g fat (6g sat. fat), 91mg chol., 766mg sod., 34g carb. (8g sugars, 6g fiber), 37g pro. **DIABETIC EXCHANGES:** 4 lean meat, 2 starch, 1 fat.

MY TWO CENT$

"This was an extremely easy and delicious dinner. The chicken was perfect. I used a chunky salsa and that worked out well. Next time I'll try something like a salsa verde. Really quick clean-up, too! Can't wait to make it again!"
—PRPLMONKY5, TASTEOFHOME.COM

ONE-POT STUFFED PEPPER DINNER

Thick like a chili and rich with stuffed-pepper flavor, this dish will warm you up on chilly days.
—Charlotte Smith, McDonald, PA

TAKES: 30 min. • **MAKES:** 4 servings

1 lb. lean ground beef (90% lean)
3 medium green peppers, chopped (about 3 cups)
3 garlic cloves, minced

2 cans (14½ oz. each) Italian diced tomatoes, undrained
2 cups water
1 can (6 oz.) tomato paste

2 Tbsp. shredded Parmesan cheese
¼ tsp. pepper
1 cup uncooked instant rice
   Additional Parmesan cheese, optional

1. In a Dutch oven, cook and crumble beef with green peppers and garlic over medium-high heat until no longer pink and peppers are tender, 5-7 minutes; drain.

2. Stir in tomatoes, water, tomato paste, 2 Tbsp. cheese and pepper; bring to a boil. Stir in rice; remove from the heat. Let stand, covered, for 5 minutes. If desired, sprinkle with additional Parmesan cheese.

2 CUPS: 415 cal., 10g fat (4g sat. fat), 72mg chol., 790mg sod., 51g carb. (20g sugars, 5g fiber), 30g pro. **DIABETIC EXCHANGES:** 3 starch, 3 lean meat.

CREAMY DIJON CHICKEN

Extremely fast and economical, this chicken dish makes a nice sauce that works well over brown rice or wide noodles. Double the recipe if you want extra sauce for leftovers.
—Irene Boffo, Fountain Hills, AZ

TAKES: 25 min. • **MAKES:** 4 servings

½ cup half-and-half cream	4 boneless skinless chicken breast halves (6 oz. each)	2 tsp. butter
¼ cup Dijon mustard	¼ tsp. salt	1 small onion, halved and very thinly sliced
1 Tbsp. brown sugar	¼ tsp. pepper	Minced fresh parsley
	2 tsp. olive oil	

1. Whisk together cream, mustard and brown sugar. Pound chicken breasts with a meat mallet to even thickness; sprinkle with salt and pepper.

2. In a large skillet, heat oil and butter over medium-high heat; brown chicken on both sides. Reduce heat to medium. Add onion and cream mixture; bring to a boil. Reduce heat; simmer, covered, until a thermometer inserted in chicken reads 165°, 10-12 minutes. Sprinkle with parsley.

1 CHICKEN BREAST HALF WITH 3 TBSP. SAUCE: 295 cal., 11g fat (5g sat. fat), 114mg chol., 621mg sod., 6g carb. (5g sugars, 0 fiber), 36g pro. **DIABETIC EXCHANGES:** 5 lean meat, 1 fat, ½ starch.

ZUCCHINI BEEF SKILLET

Turn to this speedy summer recipe when you want to use up abundant garden goodies such as zucchini, tomatoes and green peppers.
—Becky Calder, Kingston, MO

TAKES: 30 min. • **MAKES:** 4 servings

1 lb. ground beef
1 medium onion, chopped
1 small green pepper, chopped
2 tsp. chili powder
¾ tsp. salt
¼ tsp. pepper
3 medium zucchini, cut into ¾-in. cubes
2 large tomatoes, chopped
¼ cup water
1 cup uncooked instant rice
1 cup shredded cheddar cheese

1. In a large skillet, cook and crumble beef with onion and pepper over medium-high heat until no longer pink, 5-7 minutes; drain.

2. Stir in seasonings, vegetables, water and rice; bring to a boil. Reduce heat; simmer, covered, until rice is tender, 10-15 minutes. Sprinkle with cheese. Remove from heat; let stand until cheese is melted.

2 CUPS: 470 cal., 24g fat (11g sat. fat), 98mg chol., 749mg sod., 33g carb. (8g sugars, 4g fiber), 32g pro.

OUR TWO CENT$
Handle zucchini carefully; they're thin-skinned and easily damaged. To pick the freshest zucchini, look for a firm heavy squash with a moist stem end and a shiny skin. Smaller squash are generally sweeter and more tender than larger ones.

THAI PEANUT CHICKEN & NOODLES

This versatile chicken recipe is very similar to chicken pad Thai but easier to make—and it tastes just as good. Rice noodles can be swapped with mung bean noodles or any type of egg noodles.
—Kristina Segarra, Yonkers, NY

TAKES: 30 min. • **MAKES:** 4 servings

½ cup water
¼ cup soy sauce
2 Tbsp. rice vinegar
2 Tbsp. creamy peanut butter
3 garlic cloves, minced
1 to 2 tsp. Sriracha Asian hot chili sauce

1 tsp. sesame oil
1 tsp. molasses
1 pkg. (6.75 oz.) thin rice noodles
1 lb. chicken tenderloins, cut into ¾-in. pieces
2 Tbsp. peanut oil, divided

1 medium onion, chopped
Halved cucumber slices and chopped peanuts, optional

1. For sauce, whisk together the first eight ingredients. Bring a large saucepan of water to a boil; remove from heat. Add noodles; let stand until noodles are tender but firm, 3-4 minutes. Drain; rinse with cold water and drain well.

2. In a large skillet, heat 1 Tbsp. peanut oil over medium-high heat; saute chicken until no longer pink, 5-7 minutes. Remove from pan.

3. In same pan, saute onion in remaining oil over medium-high heat until tender, 2-3 minutes. Stir in sauce; cook and stir over medium heat until slightly thickened. Add noodles and chicken; heat through, tossing to combine. If desired, top with cucumber slices and chopped peanuts. Serve immediately.

2 CUPS: 444 cal., 13g fat (2g sat. fat), 56mg chol., 1270mg sod., 48g carb. (6g sugars, 2g fiber), 34g pro.

CAJUN CHICKEN & PASTA

This kicked-up pasta dish is a family favorite and my most requested recipe. It's easy to adapt, too. Swap in shrimp for the chicken, add your favorite veggies or adjust the spice level to your family's tastes. You simply can't go wrong!

—Dolly Kragel, Smithland, IA

PREP: 10 min. + standing • **COOK:** 35 min. **MAKES:** 6 servings

- 1 lb. boneless skinless chicken breasts, cut into 2x½-in. strips
- 3 tsp. Cajun seasoning
- 8 oz. uncooked penne pasta (about 2⅓ cups)
- 2 Tbsp. butter, divided
- 1 small sweet red pepper, diced
- 1 small green pepper, diced
- ½ cup sliced fresh mushrooms
- 4 green onions, chopped
- 1 cup heavy whipping cream
- ½ tsp. salt
- ¼ tsp. dried basil
- ¼ tsp. lemon-pepper seasoning
- ¼ tsp. garlic powder
  Pepper to taste
  Chopped plum tomatoes
  Minced fresh basil
  Shredded Parmesan cheese

1. Toss chicken with Cajun seasoning; let stand 15 minutes. Cook pasta according to package directions; drain.

2. In a skillet, heat 1 Tbsp. butter over medium-high heat; saute chicken until no longer pink, 5-6 minutes. Remove from pan.

3. In same pan, heat remaining butter over medium-high; saute peppers, mushrooms and green onions until the peppers are crisp-tender, 6-8 minutes. Stir in cream and seasonings; bring to a boil. Cook and stir until slightly thickened, 4-6 minutes. Stir in the pasta and chicken; heat through. Top with tomatoes and basil. Sprinkle with cheese.

1 SERVING: 398 cal., 21g fat (12g sat. fat), 97mg chol., 357mg sodium, 31g carb. (4g sugars, 2g fiber), 22g pro.

ENCHILADA CASSER-OLÉ!

My husband loves this casserole, and that's probably why it never lasts long. Packed with black beans, cheese, tomatoes and southwest flavor, it's an impressive-looking entree that's as simple as it is delicious.

—Marsha Wills, Homosassa, FL

PREP: 25 min. • **BAKE:** 30 min. • **MAKES:** 8 servings

- 1 lb. lean ground beef (90% lean)
- 1 large onion, chopped
- 2 cups salsa
- 1 can (15 oz.) black beans, rinsed and drained
- ¼ cup reduced-fat Italian salad dressing
- 2 Tbsp. reduced-sodium taco seasoning
- ¼ tsp. ground cumin
- 6 flour tortillas (8 in.)
- ¾ cup reduced-fat sour cream
- 1 cup shredded reduced-fat Mexican cheese blend
- 1 cup shredded lettuce
- 1 medium tomato, chopped
- ¼ cup minced fresh cilantro

1. In a large skillet, cook beef and onion over medium heat until meat is no longer pink; drain. Stir in the salsa, beans, dressing, taco seasoning and cumin. Place three tortillas in an 11x7-in. baking dish coated with cooking spray. Layer with half of the meat mixture, sour cream and cheese. Repeat layers.

2. Cover and bake at 400° for 25 minutes. Uncover; bake 5-10 minutes longer or until heated through. Let stand for 5 minutes; top with lettuce, tomato and cilantro.

1 PIECE: 357 cal., 12g fat (5g sat. fat), 45mg chol., 864mg sod., 37g carb. (6g sugars, 3g fiber), 23g pro. **DIABETIC EXCHANGES:** 3 lean meat, 2 starch, 1 vegetable, 1 fat.

GARLIC-GINGER TURKEY TENDERLOINS

This good-for-you entree can be on your family's plates quicker than Chinese takeout—and for a lot less money! Ginger and brown sugar flavor the sauce that spices up the turkey as it bakes.
—*Taste of Home* Test Kitchen

TAKES: 30 min. • **MAKES:** 4 servings

- 3 Tbsp. brown sugar, divided
- 2 Tbsp. plus 2 tsp. reduced-sodium soy sauce, divided
- 2 Tbsp. minced fresh gingerroot
- 6 garlic cloves, minced
- ½ tsp. pepper
- 1 pkg. (20 oz.) turkey breast tenderloins
- 1 Tbsp. cornstarch
- 1 cup reduced-sodium chicken broth

1. Preheat oven to 375°. In a small saucepan, mix 2 Tbsp. brown sugar, 2 Tbsp. soy sauce, ginger, garlic and pepper.

2. Place turkey in a 13x9-in. baking dish coated with cooking spray; drizzle with half of the soy sauce mixture. Bake, uncovered, 25-30 minutes or until a thermometer reads 165°.

3. Meanwhile, add cornstarch and the remaining brown sugar and soy sauce to the remaining mixture in saucepan; stir until smooth. Stir in broth. Bring to a boil; cook and stir 1-2 minutes or until thickened. Cut turkey into slices; serve with sauce.

4 OZ. COOKED TURKEY WITH 2 TBSP. SAUCE: 212 cal., 2g fat (1g sat. fat), 69mg chol., 639mg sod., 14g carb. (10g sugars, 0 fiber), 35g pro. **DIABETIC EXCHANGES:** 4 lean meat, 1 starch.

MY TWO CENT$

"Goes together quickly and tastes wonderful! I was slightly skeptical at first about this particular mixture of flavors, but the brown sugar balanced out the saltiness of the soy sauce and the bite of the ginger and garlic nicely. We used chicken breasts instead of turkey tenderloins and powdered ginger instead of fresh gingerroot."
—ALLISONO, TASTEOFHOME.COM

BUFFALO CHICKEN TENDERS

Chicken tenders get a spicy kick thanks to homemade Buffalo sauce. They taste like they're from a restaurant, but are so easy to make at home.
—Dahlia Abrams, Detroit, MI

TAKES: 20 min. • **MAKES:** 4 servings

- 1 lb. chicken tenderloins
- 2 Tbsp. all-purpose flour
- ¼ tsp. pepper
- 2 Tbsp. butter, divided
- ⅓ cup Louisiana-style hot sauce
- 1¼ tsp. Worcestershire sauce
- 1 tsp. minced fresh oregano
- ½ tsp. garlic powder
- Blue cheese salad dressing, optional

1. Toss chicken with flour and pepper. In a large skillet, heat 1 Tbsp. butter over medium heat. Add chicken; cook until no longer pink, about 4-6 minutes per side. Remove from pan.

2. Mix hot sauce, Worcestershire sauce, oregano and garlic powder. In same skillet, melt remaining butter; stir in sauce mixture. Add chicken; heat through, turning to coat. If desired, serve with blue cheese dressing.

1 SERVING: 184 cal., 7g fat (4g sat. fat), 71mg chol., 801mg sod., 5g carb. (1g sugars, 0 fiber), 27g pro. **DIABETIC EXCHANGES:** 3 lean meat, 1½ fat.

STUFFED PEPPERS FOR FOUR

Truly a meal in one, this quick supper has it all: veggies, meat, pasta and sauce packed into tender peppers. It looks pretty on the table, too.
—*Taste of Home* Test Kitchen

TAKES: 30 min. • **MAKES:** 4 servings

½ cup uncooked orzo pasta
4 medium sweet peppers (any color)
¼ cup water
1 lb. ground beef

½ cup chopped onion
2 cups pasta sauce
1 cup frozen broccoli-cauliflower blend, thawed and chopped

½ cup grated Parmesan cheese, divided

1. Cook orzo according to package directions; drain. Cut and discard tops from the peppers; remove seeds. Place in a 3-qt. round microwave-safe dish. Add water; microwave, covered, on high until peppers are crisp-tender, 7-9 minutes.

2. In a large skillet, cook and crumble the beef with onion over medium heat until no longer pink, 5-7 minutes; drain. Stir in the pasta sauce, vegetables, ¼ cup cheese and orzo. Spoon into peppers. Sprinkle with remaining cheese.

3. Microwave, uncovered, on high until heated through, 1-2 minutes.

1 STUFFED PEPPER: 448 cal., 18g fat (7g sat. fat), 79mg chol., 734mg sod., 41g carb. (15g sugars, 6g fiber), 30g pro.

SWEET CHILI & ORANGE CHICKEN

My husband loves this simple chicken dish, often requesting it when he comes home from deployment. The sweet chili sauce adds just the right heat to the bright, citrusy sauce.
—Jessica Eastman, Bremerton, WA

TAKES: 20 min. • **MAKES:** 4 servings

1 lb. boneless skinless chicken breasts, cut into 1-in. pieces	2 Tbsp. butter
¼ tsp. salt	¾ cup sweet chili sauce
¼ tsp. pepper	⅓ cup thawed orange juice concentrate

Hot cooked jasmine or other rice
Minced fresh basil

1. Toss chicken with salt and pepper. In a large skillet, heat butter over medium-high heat; stir-fry chicken until no longer pink, 5-7 minutes. Remove from pan; keep warm.

2. Add chili sauce and juice concentrate to skillet; cook and stir until heated through. Stir in the chicken. Serve with rice; sprinkle with basil.

½ CUP CHICKEN MIXTURE: 309 cal., 9g fat (4g sat. fat), 78mg chol., 1014mg sod., 33g carb. (31g sugars, 1g fiber), 24g pro.

OUR TWO CENT$
If you really want to crank up the heat in this recipe, use Sriracha instead of the chili sauce.

DINNER POPPERS

Talk about a recipe for success. These chicken tenders are stuffed inside peppers, wrapped in bacon and sprinkled with cheese. Cream cheese perfectly tempers the heat. My husband and son like poblanos while my daughter and I favor hotter peppers, so I mix it up to suit all of our tastes.
—Sherri Jerzyk, Tucson, AZ

PREP: 20 min. • **BAKE:** 25 min. • **MAKES:** 4 servings

4 **bacon strips**	2 **tsp. canola oil**	4 **oz. cream cheese,**
4 **chicken tenderloins**	4 **poblano peppers**	**cut into four strips**
¼ **tsp. salt**	1½ **cups shredded cheddar**	
⅛ **tsp. pepper**	**cheese, divided**	

1. Preheat oven to 350°. In a large skillet, cook bacon over medium heat until partially cooked but not crisp. Remove to paper towels to drain.

2. Sprinkle chicken with salt and pepper. In a skillet, heat oil over medium-high heat; brown tenderloins on both sides. Cool slightly.

3. Carefully cut a slit down the side of each pepper and remove seeds. Fill each with one tenderloin; top each with 2 Tbsp. cheese and a strip of cream cheese. Close peppers; wrap with bacon and secure with toothpicks.

4. Place on a foil-lined baking sheet, slit side up. Top with remaining cheddar cheese; bake until browned and peppers are tender, 25-30 minutes. Remove toothpicks before serving.

NOTE: Wear disposable gloves when cutting hot peppers; the oils can burn skin. Avoid touching your face.

1 SERVING: 389 cal., 30g fat (15g sat. fat), 96mg chol., 682mg sod., 9g carb. (4g sugars, 2g fiber), 23g pro.

SOUTHWESTERN CASSEROLE

I've been making this mild family-pleasing casserole for years. It tastes delicious, fits nicely into our budget and, best of all, the recipe makes a second one to freeze and enjoy later.
—Joan Hallford, North Richland Hills, TX

PREP: 15 min. • **BAKE:** 40 min. • **MAKES:** 2 casseroles (6 servings each)

- 2 cups (8 oz.) uncooked elbow macaroni
- 2 lbs. ground beef
- 1 large onion, chopped
- 2 garlic cloves, minced
- 2 cans (14½ oz. each) diced tomatoes, undrained

- 1 can (16 oz.) kidney beans, rinsed and drained
- 1 can (6 oz.) tomato paste
- 1 can (4 oz.) chopped green chilies, drained
- 1½ tsp. salt
- 1 tsp. chili powder

- ½ tsp. ground cumin
- ½ tsp. pepper
- 2 cups shredded Monterey Jack cheese
- 2 jalapeno peppers, seeded and chopped

1. Cook macaroni according to the package directions. Meanwhile, in a large saucepan, cook beef and onion over medium heat, crumbling beef, until meat is no longer pink. Add garlic; cook 1 minute longer. Drain. Stir in next eight ingredients. Bring to a boil. Reduce heat; simmer, uncovered, for 10 minutes. Drain macaroni; stir into beef mixture.

2. Preheat oven to 375°. Transfer macaroni mixture to two greased 2-qt. baking dishes. Top with cheese and jalapenos. Cover and bake at 375° for 30 minutes. Uncover; bake until bubbly and heated through, about 10 minutes longer. Serve one casserole. Cool the second; cover and freeze up to 3 months.

FREEZE OPTION: To use frozen casserole, thaw in the refrigerator 8 hours. Preheat oven to 375°. Remove from the refrigerator 30 minutes before baking. Cover and bake, increasing bake time as necessary to heat through and for a thermometer inserted in center to read 165°, 20-25 minutes.

NOTE: Wear disposable gloves when cutting hot peppers; the oils can burn skin. Avoid touching your face.

1 CUP: 321 cal., 15g fat (7g sat. fat), 64mg chol., 673mg sod., 23g carb. (5g sugars, 4g fiber), 24g pro.

SAUSAGE-STUFFED BUTTERNUT SQUASH

Load butternut squash shells with an Italian turkey sausage and squash mixture for a quick and easy meal. The best part? This recipe is surprisingly low in calories.
—Katia Slinger, West Jordan, UT

TAKES: 30 min. • **MAKES:** 4 servings

- 1 medium butternut squash (about 3 lbs.)
- 1 lb. Italian turkey sausage links, casings removed
- 1 medium onion, finely chopped
- 4 garlic cloves, minced
- ½ cup shredded Italian cheese blend
   Crushed red pepper flakes, optional

1. Preheat broiler. Cut squash lengthwise in half; discard seeds. Place the squash in a large microwave-safe dish, cut side down; add ½ in. of water. Microwave, covered, on high until soft, 20-25 minutes. Cool slightly.

2. Meanwhile, in a large nonstick skillet, cook and crumble sausage with onion over medium-high heat until no longer pink, 5-7 minutes. Add garlic; cook and stir 1 minute.

3. Leaving ½-in.-thick shells, scoop pulp from squash and stir into sausage mixture. Place squash shells on a baking sheet; fill with sausage mixture. Sprinkle with cheese.

4. Broil 4-5 in. from heat until cheese is melted, 1-2 minutes. If desired, sprinkle with pepper flakes. To serve, cut each half into two portions.

1 SERVING: 325 cal., 10g fat (4g sat. fat), 52mg chol., 587mg sod., 44g carb. (10g sugars, 12g fiber), 19g pro. **DIABETIC EXCHANGES:** 3 starch, 3 lean meat.

HEALTH TIP: Butternut squash is an excellent source of vitamin A in the form of beta-carotene. It's important for normal vision and a healthy immune system, and it helps the heart, lungs and kidneys function properly.

Affordable Entrees:
PORK, SEAFOOD & MEATLESS

If the usual dinner rotation is starting to feel stodgy, shake things up with succulent pork, fresh fish and seafood, or veggie-packed meatless meals. The only thing better than the versatility and utter deliciousness of these recipes is the extra money left in your pocket.

BLACKENED TILAPIA WITH ZUCCHINI NOODLES

I love quick and bright meals like this one-skillet wonder. Homemade pico de gallo is easy to make the night before.

—Tammy Brownlow, Dallas, TX

TAKES: 30 min. • **MAKES:** 4 servings

2 large zucchini (about 1½ lbs.)
1½ tsp. ground cumin
¾ tsp. salt, divided
½ tsp. smoked paprika
½ tsp. pepper
¼ tsp garlic powder
4 tilapia fillets (6 oz. each)
2 tsp. olive oil
2 garlic cloves, minced
1 cup pico de gallo

1. Trim ends of zucchini. Using a spiralizer, cut zucchini into thin strands.

2. Mix cumin, ½ tsp. salt, smoked paprika, pepper and garlic powder; sprinkle generously onto both sides of tilapia. In a large nonstick skillet, heat oil over medium-high heat. In batches, cook tilapia until fish just begins to flake easily with a fork, 2-3 minutes per side. Remove from pan; keep warm.

3. In same pan, cook zucchini with garlic over medium-high heat until slightly softened, 1-2 minutes, tossing constantly with tongs (do not overcook). Sprinkle with remaining salt. Serve with tilapia and pico de gallo. If a spiralizer is not available, zucchini may also be cut into ribbons using a vegetable peeler. Saute as directed, increasing time as necessary.

1 SERVING: 203 cal., 4g fat (1g sat. fat), 83mg chol., 522mg sod., 8g carb. (5g sugars, 2g fiber), 34g pro. **DIABETIC EXCHANGES:** 5 lean meat, 1 vegetable, ½ fat.

BACON-WRAPPED PESTO PORK TENDERLOIN

We love to serve this family-favorite tenderloin—probably because of the compliments that come with it! When the weather warms up, we grill it outdoors instead of roasting it in the oven.
—Megan Riofski, Frankfort, IL

PREP: 30 min. • **BAKE:** 20 min. • **MAKES:** 4 servings

- 10 bacon strips
- 1 pork tenderloin (1 lb.)
- ¼ tsp. pepper
- ⅓ cup prepared pesto
- 1 cup shredded Italian cheese blend
- 1 cup fresh baby spinach

1. Preheat oven to 425°. Arrange the bacon strips lengthwise in a foil-lined 15x10x1-in. pan, overlapping slightly.

2. Cut tenderloin lengthwise through the center to within ½ in. of bottom. Open tenderloin flat; cover with plastic wrap. Pound with a meat mallet to ½-in. thickness. Remove plastic; place tenderloin on center of bacon, perpendicular to the strips.

3. Sprinkle pepper over pork. Spread with pesto; layer with cheese and spinach. Close tenderloin; wrap with bacon, overlapping ends. Tie with kitchen string at 3-in. intervals. Secure ends with toothpicks.

4. In a 12-in. skillet, brown roast on all sides, about 8 minutes. Return to baking pan; roast in oven until a thermometer inserted in the pork reads 145°, 17-20 minutes. Remove string and toothpicks; let stand 5 minutes before slicing.

1 SERVING: 402 cal., 25g fat (9g sat. fat), 104mg chol., 864mg sod., 4g carb. (1g sugars, 1g fiber), 37g pro.

SAUSAGE & SPINACH CALZONES

These comforting calzones are perfect for quick meals—or even a midnight snack. My nurse co-workers always ask me to make them when it's my turn to bring in lunch.
—Kourtney Williams, Mechanicsville, VA

TAKES: 30 min. • **MAKES:** 4 servings

½ lb. bulk Italian sausage
3 cups fresh baby spinach
1 tube (13.8 oz.) refrigerated pizza crust

¾ cup shredded part-skim mozzarella cheese
½ cup part-skim ricotta cheese

¼ tsp. pepper
Pizza sauce, optional

1. Preheat oven to 400°. In a large skillet, cook and crumble sausage over medium heat until no longer pink, 4-6 minutes; drain. Add spinach; cook and stir until wilted. Remove from heat.

2. On a lightly floured surface, unroll and pat dough into a 15x11-in. rectangle. Cut into four rectangles. Sprinkle mozzarella cheese on one half of each rectangle to within 1 in. of edges.

3. Stir ricotta cheese and pepper into sausage mixture; spoon over mozzarella cheese. Fold dough over filling; press edges with a fork to seal. Place on a greased baking sheet.

4. Bake until light golden brown, 10-15 minutes. If desired, serve with pizza sauce.

FREEZE OPTION: Freeze cooled calzones in an airtight freezer container. To use, microwave calzone on high until heated through.

1 CALZONE: 489 cal., 22g fat (9g sat. fat), 54mg chol., 1242mg sod., 51g carb. (7g sugars, 2g fiber), 23g pro.

SKILLET HAM & RICE

Ham, rice and mushrooms make a tasty combination in this homey stovetop dish. It goes from start to finish in just 25 minutes.
—Susan Zivec, Regina, SK

TAKES: 25 min. • **MAKES:** 2 servings

- 1 tsp. olive oil
- 1 medium onion, chopped
- 1 cup sliced fresh mushrooms
- 1 cup cubed fully cooked ham
- ⅛ tsp. pepper
- ½ cup reduced-sodium chicken broth
- ¼ cup water
- ¾ cup uncooked instant rice
- 2 green onions, sliced
- ¼ cup shredded Parmesan cheese

1. In a large nonstick skillet, heat the oil over medium-high heat; saute onion and mushrooms until tender. Stir in the ham, pepper, broth and water; bring to a boil. Stir in rice. Reduce heat; simmer, covered, until the rice is tender, about 5 minutes.

2. Fluff with a fork. Top with green onions and Parmesan cheese.

1¼ CUPS: 322 cal., 8g fat (3g sat. fat), 49mg chol., 1168mg sod., 38g carb. (4g sugars, 2g fiber), 24g pro.

HEALTH TIP: Look for lower-sodium versions of ham in the meat and deli sections. They typically have 25-30 percent less sodium.

GARLIC LEMON SHRIMP

This shrimp pasta is amazingly quick. Make extra sauce so you can soak it up with crusty bread.
—Athena Russell, Greenville, SC

TAKES: 20 min. • **MAKES:** 4 servings

2	Tbsp. olive oil
1	lb. uncooked shrimp (26-30 per lb.), peeled and deveined

3	garlic cloves, thinly sliced
1	Tbsp. lemon juice
1	tsp. ground cumin
¼	tsp. salt

2	Tbsp. minced fresh parsley
	Hot cooked pasta or rice

In a large skillet, heat oil over medium-high heat; saute shrimp 3 minutes. Add garlic, lemon juice, cumin and salt; cook and stir until shrimp turn pink. Stir in parsley. Serve with pasta.

HEALTH TIP: Cooking the shrimp in olive oil instead of butter saves about 3 grams saturated fat per serving.

1 SERVING: 163 cal., 8g fat (1g sat. fat), 138mg chol., 284mg sod., 2g carb. (0 sugars, 0 fiber), 19g pro. **DIABETIC EXCHANGES:** 3 lean meat, 1½ fat.

MY TWO CENT$

"Easy and tasty! We enjoyed this recipe. Next time I will use less cumin and double the sauce. Will definitely make this again and again!"
—NHBABE, TASTEOFHOME.COM

BEER PORK CHOPS

These tender chops cooked in a savory sauce are perfect for a hectic weeknight because they're easy to prep and only use a few ingredients. Try them with hot, buttery noodles.
—Jana Christian, Farson, WY

TAKES: 20 min. • **MAKES:** 4 servings

- 4 boneless pork loin chops (4 oz. each)
- ½ tsp. salt
- ½ tsp. pepper
- 1 Tbsp. canola oil
- 3 Tbsp. ketchup
- 2 Tbsp. brown sugar
- ¾ cup beer or nonalcoholic beer

1. Sprinkle pork chops with salt and pepper. In a large skillet, heat oil over medium heat; brown chops on both sides.

2. Mix the ketchup, brown sugar and beer; pour over chops. Bring to a boil. Reduce heat; simmer, uncovered, until a thermometer inserted in pork reads 145°, 4-6 minutes. Let stand 5 minutes before serving.

FREEZE OPTION: Place pork chops in freezer containers; top with sauce. Cool and freeze. To use, partially thaw in refrigerator overnight. Heat through in a covered saucepan, gently stirring sauce and adding a little water if necessary.

1 PORK CHOP: 239 cal., 10g fat (3g sat. fat), 55mg chol., 472mg sod., 11g carb. (11g sugars, 0 fiber), 22g pro. **DIABETIC EXCHANGES:** 3 lean meat, 1 fat, ½ starch.

BLACK BEAN & SWEET POTATO RICE BOWLS

With three hungry boys in my house, dinners need to be quick and filling, and it helps to get in some veggies, too. This one is a favorite because it's hearty and fun to tweak with different ingredients.
—Kim Van Dunk, Caldwell, NJ

TAKES: 30 min. • **MAKES:** 4 servings

- ¾ cup uncooked long grain rice
- ¼ tsp. garlic salt
- 1½ cups water
- 3 Tbsp. olive oil, divided
- 1 large sweet potato, peeled and diced

- 1 medium red onion, finely chopped
- 4 cups chopped fresh kale (tough stems removed)
- 1 can (15 oz.) black beans, rinsed and drained

- 2 Tbsp. sweet chili sauce
  Lime wedges, optional
  Additional sweet chili sauce, optional

1. Place the rice, garlic salt and water in a large saucepan; bring to a boil. Reduce heat; simmer, covered, until water is absorbed and the rice is tender, 15-20 minutes. Remove from heat; let stand 5 minutes.

2. Meanwhile, in a large skillet, heat 2 Tbsp. olive oil over medium-high heat; saute sweet potato for 8 minutes. Add the onion; cook and stir until potato is tender, 4-6 minutes. Add kale; cook and stir until tender, 3-5 minutes. Stir in beans; heat through.

3. Gently stir 2 Tbsp. chili sauce and remaining oil into rice; add to potato mixture. If desired, serve with lime wedges and additional chili sauce.

2 CUPS: 435 cal., 11g fat (2g sat. fat), 0 chol., 405mg sod., 74g carb. (15g sugars, 8g fiber), 10g pro.

PEPPERED PORK PITAS

Cracked black pepper is all it takes to give my pork pitas some pop. Then I fill them with caramelized onions and garlic mayo. With these, any weeknight is awesome.
—Katherine White, Henderson, NV

TAKES: 20 min. • **MAKES:** 4 servings

- 1 lb. boneless pork loin chops, cut into thin strips
- 1 Tbsp. olive oil
- 2 tsp. coarsely ground pepper
- 2 garlic cloves, minced
- 1 jar (12 oz.) roasted sweet peppers, drained and julienned
- 4 whole pita breads, warmed
  Garlic mayonnaise and torn leaf lettuce, optional

In a small bowl, combine pork strips, oil, pepper and garlic; toss to coat. Place a large skillet over medium-high heat. Add pork mixture; cook and stir until no longer pink. Stir in sweet peppers; heat through. Serve on pita breads. Top with the mayonnaise and lettuce if desired.

1 SANDWICH: 380 cal., 11g fat (3g sat. fat), 55mg chol., 665mg sod., 37g carb. (4g sugars, 2g fiber), 27g pro. **DIABETIC EXCHANGES:** 3 lean meat, 2 starch, 1 fat.

OUR TWO CENT$

Unlike beef, cuts of pork vary little in tenderness. Use dry-heat cooking methods (broiling, grilling, pan-broiling, roasting and stir-frying) when a firm texture is desired. Moist-heat braising is used when a fork-tender texture is desired.

PESTO CORN SALAD WITH SHRIMP

Showcase the beautiful bounty of summer with fresh corn, tomatoes and basil in this delicious salad. Prevent browning by spritzing the salad with lemon juice.
—Deena Bowen, Chico, CA

TAKES: 30 min. • **MAKES:** 4 servings

- 4 medium ears sweet corn, husks removed
- ½ cup packed fresh basil leaves
- ¼ cup olive oil
- ½ tsp. salt, divided
- 1½ cups cherry tomatoes, halved
- ⅛ tsp. pepper
- 1 medium ripe avocado, peeled and chopped
- 1 lb. uncooked shrimp (31-40 per lb.), peeled and deveined

1. In a pot of boiling water, cook corn until tender, about 5 minutes. Drain; cool slightly. Meanwhile, in a food processor, pulse basil, oil and ¼ tsp. salt until blended.

2. Cut corn from cob and place in a bowl. Stir in tomatoes, pepper and remaining salt. Add the avocado and 2 Tbsp. basil mixture; toss gently to combine.

3. Thread shrimp onto metal or soaked wooden skewers; brush with remaining basil mixture. Grill, covered, over medium heat until shrimp turn pink, 2-4 minutes per side. Remove shrimp from skewers; serve with corn mixture.

1 SERVING: 371 cal., 22g fat (3g sat. fat), 138mg chol., 450mg sod., 25g carb. (8g sugars, 5g fiber), 23g pro.

SKILLET MAC & CHEESE

This skillet mac and cheese is so simple and so full of melty, cheesy goodness, it almost seems too good to be true. It's a fantastic dish for kids, but you can also dress it up with arugula and cherry tomatoes to give it grown-up appeal.
—Ann Bowers, Rockport, TX

TAKES: 25 min. • **MAKES:** 4 servings

2 cups uncooked elbow macaroni (about 8 oz.)
2 Tbsp. butter
2 Tbsp. all-purpose flour
1½ cups half-and-half cream
¾ lb. process cheese (Velveeta), cubed
Fresh arugula, halved cherry tomatoes and coarsely ground pepper, optional

1. Cook macaroni according to package directions; drain.

2. Meanwhile, in a large nonstick skillet, melt butter over medium heat. Stir in the flour until smooth; gradually whisk in cream. Bring to a boil, stirring constantly. Cook and stir until thickened, about 2 minutes. Reduce the heat; stir in cheese until melted.

3. Add macaroni; cook and stir until heated through. Top as desired.

1½ CUPS: 600 cal., 37g fat (23g sat. fat), 144mg chol., 1185mg sod., 40g carb. (9g sugars, 1g fiber), 23g pro.

ZESTY GRILLED HAM

If it's ham, my kids will eat it, and they like this kicked-up recipe best of all. Even the small ones eat adult-sized portions, so be sure to make plenty.
—Mary Ann Lien, Tyler, TX

TAKES: 15 min. • **MAKES:** 4 servings

⅓ cup packed brown sugar

2 Tbsp. prepared horseradish

4 tsp. lemon juice

1 fully cooked bone-in ham steak (1 lb.)

1. Place brown sugar, horseradish and lemon juice in a small saucepan; bring to a boil, stirring constantly. Brush over both sides of ham.

2. Place ham on an oiled grill rack over medium heat. Grill, covered, until glazed and heated through, 7-10 minutes, turning occasionally.

1 SERVING: 180 cal., 5g fat (2g sat. fat), 44mg chol., 845mg sod., 20g carb. (19g sugars, 0 fiber), 14g pro.

MY TWO CENT$

"This glaze is so simple yet so good. It is our favorite for grilled ham slices. We love it."
—LUSZOO1, TASTEOFHOME.COM

BROILED COD

Here is the easiest and tastiest cod you've ever had. Even finicky eaters who don't favor fish will love the beautiful and flaky results.
—Kim Russell, North Wales, PA

TAKES: 30 min. • **MAKES:** 2 servings

¼ cup fat-free Italian
 salad dressing
½ tsp. sugar
⅛ tsp. salt

⅛ tsp. garlic powder
⅛ tsp. curry powder
⅛ tsp. paprika
⅛ tsp. pepper

2 cod fillets (6 oz. each)
2 tsp. butter

1. Preheat broiler. In a shallow bowl, mix first seven ingredients; add cod, turning to coat. Let stand 10-15 minutes.

2. Place fillets on a greased rack of a broiler pan; discard remaining marinade. Broil 3-4 in. from heat until fish just begins to flake easily with a fork, 10-12 minutes. Top with butter.

1 FILLET: 168 cal., 5g fat (3g sat. fat), 75mg chol., 365mg sod., 2g carb. (2g sugars, 0 fiber), 27g pro. **DIABETIC EXCHANGES:** 4 lean meat, 1 fat.

CURRIED SHRIMP PASTA

Light and spicy shrimp dish pair beautifully with tender pasta and crisp sugar snaps. I usually use capellini pasta, but angel hair works, too.
—Thomas Faglon, Somerset, NJ

TAKES: 25 min. • **MAKES:** 4 servings

- 8 oz. uncooked angel hair pasta
- 8 oz. fresh sugar snap peas (about 2 cups), halved diagonally
- 2 Tbsp. olive oil
- 1 lb. uncooked shrimp (26-30 per lb.), peeled and deveined
- 3 tsp. curry powder
- 1 tsp. ground cumin
- ¾ tsp. salt
- 6 green onions, diagonally sliced

1. Cook pasta according to package directions, adding snap peas during the last 1-2 minutes of cooking. Drain, reserving ½ cup pasta water.

2. In a large skillet, heat oil over medium-high heat; saute shrimp 2 minutes. Add seasonings and green onions; cook and stir until shrimp turns pink, 1-2 minutes. Add pasta and peas; heat through, tossing to combine and adding reserved pasta water if desired.

1⅓ CUPS: 404 cal., 10g fat (1g sat. fat), 138mg chol., 588mg sod., 50g carb. (4g sugars, 5g fiber), 28g pro. **DIABETIC EXCHANGES:** 3 starch, 3 lean meat, 1½ fat.

TORTELLINI CARBONARA

Bacon, cream and Parmesan cheese combine for a creamy sauce that's heavenly poured over pasta. Keep this easy recipe in your back pocket for the next time last-minute company drops by.
—Cathy Croyle, Davidsville, PA

TAKES: 20 min. • **MAKES:** 4 servings

1 pkg. (9 oz.) refrigerated cheese tortellini
8 bacon strips, chopped
1 cup heavy whipping cream
½ cup grated Parmesan cheese
½ cup chopped fresh parsley

1. Cook tortellini according to the package directions; drain.

2. Meanwhile, in a large skillet, cook bacon over medium heat until crisp, stirring occasionally. Remove with a slotted spoon; drain on paper towels. Pour off drippings.

3. In same pan, combine cream, cheese, parsley and bacon; heat through over medium heat. Stir in tortellini. Serve immediately.

1 CUP: 527 cal., 36g fat (20g sat. fat), 121mg chol., 728mg sod., 33g carb. (3g sugars, 2g fiber), 19g pro.

OUR TWO CENT$
Traditional carbonara often has eggs in the sauce. If you'd like to add a little extra protein, halve the cream in this recipe and temper two whisked eggs into the sauce. To temper eggs, gradually add a small amount of the hot cream mixture to two whisked eggs before adding it all back to the pan. Be sure to do this after removing the pan from the heat to keep the eggs from getting too hot too quickly, which could result in scrambling.

SMART SIDE DISHES

A memorable menu just isn't complete without on-the-side sensations that complement the main course. Here you'll find an economical selection of veggies, bread, rice, potatoes and more.

SEASONED FRIES

Instead of making french fries from scratch, I reach for frozen spuds and dress them up with Parmesan cheese and Italian seasoning. They're always popular with my family.
—Maribeth Edwards, Follansbee, WV

TAKES: 15 min. • **MAKES:** 6 servings

- 6 cups frozen shoestring potatoes
- ½ cup grated Parmesan cheese
- 2 tsp. Italian seasoning
- ½ tsp. salt

Place potatoes on a foil-lined baking sheet. Bake at 450° for 8 minutes. Combine the remaining ingredients; sprinkle over potatoes and mix gently. Bake 4-5 minutes longer or until the potatoes are browned and crisp.

OUR TWO CENT$

Italian seasoning can be found in the spice aisle of most grocery stores. A basic blend might contain marjoram, thyme, rosemary, savory, sage, oregano and basil. If your grocery store does not carry Italian seasoning, ask the manager if it can be ordered. Or, mix up your own. If you don't have all the ingredients on your spice shelf, you can blend just a few of them with good results. Try substituting ¼ teaspoon each of basil, thyme, rosemary and oregano for each teaspoon of Italian seasoning called for in a recipe.

PARMESAN ROASTED BROCCOLI

Sure, it's simple and healthy but, oh, is this roasted broccoli delicious. Cutting the stalks into tall trees turns this ordinary veggie into a standout side dish.
—Holly Sander, Lake Mary, FL

TAKES: 30 min. • **MAKES:** 4 servings

- 2 small broccoli crowns (about 8 oz. each)
- 3 Tbsp. olive oil
- ½ tsp. salt
- ½ tsp. pepper
- ¼ tsp. crushed red pepper flakes
- 4 garlic cloves, thinly sliced
- 2 Tbsp. grated Parmesan cheese
- 1 tsp. grated lemon zest

1. Preheat oven to 425°. Cut the broccoli crowns into quarters from top to bottom. Drizzle with oil; sprinkle with seasonings. Place broccoli in a parchment-lined 15x10x1-in. pan.

2. Roast until crisp-tender, 10-12 minutes. Sprinkle with garlic; roast 5 minutes. Sprinkle with cheese; roast until cheese is melted and stalks of broccoli are tender, 2-4 minutes more. Sprinkle with lemon zest.

2 BROCCOLI PIECES: 144 cal., 11g fat (2g sat. fat), 2mg chol., 378mg sod., 9g carb. (2g sugars, 3g fiber), 4g pro. **DIABETIC EXCHANGES:** 2 fat, 1 vegetable.

RED WINE CRANBERRY SAUCE

We were feeling festive when we started our holiday cooking, but a full bottle of wine was a bit more than we wanted to drink. So I added half a cup to the cranberry sauce, in place of juice, and a new recipe was born!

—Helen Nelander, Boulder Creek, CA

PREP: 5 min. • **COOK:** 20 min. + chilling • **MAKES:** about 2⅓ cups

- 1 pkg. (12 oz.) fresh or frozen cranberries
- 1 cup sugar
- 1 cup water
- ½ cup dry red wine or grape juice

1. In a large saucepan, combine all ingredients; bring to a boil, stirring to dissolve sugar. Reduce heat to medium; cook, uncovered, until most of the berries pop, about 15 minutes, stirring occasionally.

2. Transfer to a bowl; cool slightly. Refrigerate, covered, until cold (sauce will thicken upon cooling).

¼ CUP: 122 cal., 0 fat (0 sat. fat), 0 chol., 1mg sod., 30g carb. (27g sugars, 2g fiber), 0 pro.

OUR TWO CENT$

Red wine makes this cranberry sauce a little more tart and less sweet than others of its kind. We tested this recipe with cabernet sauvignon, but you could also use merlot, pinot noir or sangiovese.

HERB-HAPPY GARLIC BREAD

You'll love the fresh garlic and herbs in this recipe. The crumbled goat cheese that's sprinkled on top makes it extra rich.
—*Taste of Home* Test Kitchen

TAKES: 15 min. • **MAKES:** 12 servings

- ½ cup butter, softened
- ¼ cup grated Romano cheese
- 2 Tbsp. minced fresh basil or 2 tsp. dried basil
- 1 Tbsp. minced fresh parsley
- 3 garlic cloves, minced
- 1 French bread baguette
- 4 oz. crumbled goat cheese

1. In a small bowl, mix the first five ingredients until blended. Cut baguette crosswise in half; cut each piece lengthwise in half. Spread the cut sides with butter mixture. Place on an ungreased baking sheet.

2. Bake, uncovered, at 425° until lightly toasted, 7-9 minutes. Sprinkle with goat cheese; bake until goat cheese is softened, 1-2 minutes longer. Cut into slices.

1 SLICE: 169 cal., 11g fat (7g sat. fat), 35mg chol., 307mg sod., 14g carb. (0 sugars, 1g fiber), 5g pro.

MY TWO CENT$

"This is excellent! I've made this twice for family and friends, and it was loved by everyone. When I am short on time I mix the butter a day in advance to make dinner prep just a little faster!"
—XXCSKIER, TASTEOFHOME.COM

LEMON GARLIC MUSHROOMS

I baste whole mushrooms with a lemony sauce to prepare this simple side dish. Using skewers or a basket makes it easy to turn them as they grill to perfection.
—Diane Hixon, Niceville, FL

TAKES: 15 min. • **MAKES:** 4 servings

¼ cup lemon juice
3 Tbsp. minced fresh parsley

2 Tbsp. olive oil
3 garlic cloves, minced
Pepper to taste

1 lb. large fresh mushrooms

1. For dressing, whisk together first five ingredients. Toss mushrooms with 2 Tbsp. dressing.

2. Grill mushrooms, covered, over medium-high heat until tender, 5-7 minutes per side. Toss with remaining dressing before serving.

1 SERVING: 94 cal., 7g fat (1g sat. fat), 0 chol., 2mg sod., 6g carb. (0 sugars, 0 fiber), 3g pro. **DIABETIC EXCHANGES:** 1½ fat, 1 vegetable.

NO-FUSS ROLLS

These four-ingredient rolls are ready in no time. And they taste great with herb butter or jam.
—Glenda Trail, Manchester, TN

TAKES: 25 min. • **MAKES:** 6 rolls

1 cup self-rising flour

½ cup 2% milk
2 Tbsp. mayonnaise

½ tsp. sugar

In a small bowl, combine all of the ingredients. Spoon into six muffin cups coated with cooking spray. Bake at 450° until a toothpick comes out clean, 12-14 minutes. Cool for 5 minutes before removing from pan to a wire rack. Serve warm.

NOTE: As a substitute for 1 cup of self-rising flour, place 1½ tsp. baking powder and ½ tsp. salt in a measuring cup. Add all-purpose flour to measure 1 cup.

1 SERVING: 111 cal., 4g fat (1g sat. fat), 3mg chol., 275mg sod., 16g carb. (1g sugars, 0 fiber), 3g pro. **DIABETIC EXCHANGES:** 1 starch, 1 fat.

BRAISED DILL POTATOES

Dill, chicken broth and a few other simple ingredients combine to create a side dish your family will love. The braised potatoes are delicious with sour cream.
—Amie Schmidt, San Diego, CA

TAKES: 30 min. • **MAKES:** 4 servings

1 lb. fingerling potatoes	1 Tbsp. butter	⅛ tsp. pepper
1 cup chicken broth	3 Tbsp. snipped fresh dill	2 Tbsp. sour cream
	⅛ tsp. salt	

1. In a large saucepan, arrange potatoes in a single layer. Add broth and butter. Cover and cook over medium-high heat for 12 minutes.

2. Uncover; cook until potatoes are tender and broth is evaporated, 7-10 minutes. Press each potato with a turner to crush slightly. Sprinkle evenly with the dill, salt and pepper. Cook until bottoms are lightly browned, 2-3 minutes longer. Serve with sour cream.

1 SERVING: 117 cal., 4g fat (3g sat. fat), 14mg chol., 345mg sod., 15g carb. (1g sugars, 2g fiber), 3g pro. **DIABETIC EXCHANGES:** 1 starch, 1 fat.

MY TWO CENT$

"I love potatoes, and I'll eat them any way I can, but I'd never had braised for some reason. This recipe was perfect exposure to my new favorite way to eat my favorite side. Very easy and quick recipe, and very tasty results!"

—GINA.KAPFHAMER, TASTEOFHOME.COM

SPINACH RICE

I like to serve this Greek-style rice dish alongside steaks with mushrooms. It makes an elegant meal that can be doubled for guests.
—Jeanette Cakouros, Brunswick, ME

TAKES: 20 min. • **MAKES:** 2 servings

2 Tbsp. olive oil
½ cup chopped onion
¾ cup water

1 Tbsp. dried parsley flakes
¼ to ½ tsp. salt
⅛ tsp. pepper

½ cup uncooked instant rice
2 cups fresh baby spinach

1. In a saucepan, heat oil over medium-high heat; saute onion until tender. Stir in water, parsley, salt and pepper; bring to a boil. Stir in rice; top with spinach.

2. Cover; remove from heat. Let stand until rice is tender, 7-10 minutes. Stir to combine.

¾ **CUP:** 235 cal., 14g fat (2g sat. fat), 0 chol., 326mg sod., 25g carb. (2g sugars, 2g fiber), 3g pro. **DIABETIC EXCHANGES:** 3 fat, 1½ starch, 1 vegetable.

ONE-DISH NO-KNEAD BREAD

Here's an easy way to have homemade bread with dinner tonight. Don't worry if you're new to baking. Anyone who can stir can make this a success!
—Heather Chambers, Largo, FL

PREP: 15 min. + rising • **BAKE:** 40 min. • **MAKES:** 1 loaf (12 slices)

1 tsp. active dry yeast	2¾ cups all-purpose flour	2 Tbsp. olive oil
1½ cups warm water (110° to 115°)	2 Tbsp. sugar	1½ tsp. salt

1. In a large bowl, dissolve yeast in warm water. Stir in remaining ingredients to form a wet dough; transfer to a greased 2½-qt. baking dish. Cover; let stand in a warm place 1 hour.

2. Stir down dough. Cover; let stand 1 hour. Preheat oven to 425°.

3. Bake 20 minutes. Reduce oven setting to 350°. Bake until the top of bread is golden brown and a thermometer reads 210°, about 20 minutes.

4. Remove bread from baking dish to a wire rack to cool. Serve warm.

1 SLICE: 133 cal., 3g fat (0 sat. fat), 0 chol., 296mg sod., 24g carb. (2g sugars, 1g fiber), 3g pro. **DIABETIC EXCHANGES:** 1½ starch, ½ fat.

ZUCCHINI MUSHROOM BAKE

Just a 10-minute prep dresses up my garden-fresh zucchini with mushrooms, onion, cheddar and a sprinkle of basil.
—Jacquelyn Smith, Carmel, ME

PREP: 10 min. • **BAKE:** 30 min. • **MAKES:** 4 servings

3 cups sliced zucchini
2 cups sliced fresh mushrooms

⅓ cup sliced onion
½ tsp. dried basil
¼ tsp. salt

½ cup shredded cheddar cheese

1. Preheat oven to 350°. Toss together first five ingredients; place in a shallow greased 2-qt. baking dish.

2. Bake, covered, 30 minutes. Sprinkle with cheese; bake, uncovered, until vegetables are tender, about 10 minutes.

⅔ CUP: 83 cal., 5g fat (3g sat. fat), 14mg chol., 249mg sod., 5g carb. (3g sugars, 1g fiber), 5g pro. **DIABETIC EXCHANGES:** 1 medium-fat meat, 1 vegetable.

LORA'S RED BEANS & RICE

My dear mother-in-law passed this simple recipe to me. With meats, beans and savory veggies that simmer all day, it's tasty, easy and economical, too!
—Carol Simms, Madison, MS

PREP: 15 min. + soaking • **COOK:** 8 hours • **MAKES:** 10 servings

1 pkg. (16 oz.) dried kidney beans (about 2½ cups)
2 cups cubed fully cooked ham (about 1 lb.)
1 pkg. (12 oz.) fully cooked andouille chicken sausage links or flavor of choice, sliced
1 medium green pepper, chopped
1 medium onion, chopped
2 celery ribs, chopped
1 Tbsp. hot pepper sauce
2 garlic cloves, minced
1½ tsp. salt
Hot cooked rice

1. Place beans in a large bowl; add cool water to cover. Soak overnight.

2. Drain beans, discarding water; rinse with cool water. Place beans in a greased 6-qt. slow cooker. Stir in ham, sausage, vegetables, pepper sauce, garlic and salt. Add water to cover by 1 in.

3. Cook, covered, on low until beans are tender, 8-9 hours. Serve with rice.

1 CUP BEAN MIXTURE: 249 cal., 5g fat (1g sat. fat), 43mg chol., 906mg sod., 31g carb. (2g sugars, 7g fiber), 23g pro.

OUR TWO CENT$
Feel free to substitute smoked turkey sausage for the andouille.

AU GRATIN PEAS & POTATOES

While this delicious potato skillet is a wonderful side dish, we find it satisfying enough to be a main course, too. The skillet preparation takes less time than baking an au gratin casserole or scalloped potatoes—but it's still good old-fashioned comfort food at its best!
—Marie Peterson, DeForest, WI

TAKES: 30 min. • **MAKES:** 6 servings

- 6 bacon strips, diced
- 1 medium onion, chopped
- 4 cups sliced peeled cooked potatoes
- ½ tsp. salt
- 1 pkg. (10 oz.) frozen peas, cooked and drained
- 2 cups shredded sharp cheddar cheese, divided
- ½ cup mayonnaise
- ½ cup whole milk

1. In a large skillet, cook bacon until crisp. Remove with a slotted spoon to paper towels. Drain, reserving 1 Tbsp. drippings. In the drippings, saute onion until tender.

2. Layer with potatoes, salt, peas, 1 cup of cheese and bacon. Reduce heat; cover and simmer for 10 minutes or until heated through.

3. Combine mayonnaise and milk until smooth; pour over bacon. Sprinkle with the remaining cheese. Remove from the heat; let stand for 5 minutes before serving.

1 CUP: 473 cal., 31g fat (11g sat. fat), 52mg chol., 794mg sod., 31g carb. (5g sugars, 4g fiber), 18g pro.

SOUPS, SALADS & SAMMIES

A warm soup, hearty sandwich or tasty salad can make supper sing—or serve as a light meal all by itself. Look here for an assortment of fresh and flavorful options.

HUMMUS & VEGGIE WRAP-UP

I had a sandwich similar to this once at a diner while on a long and arduous walk. I enjoyed it so much that I modified it to my own taste and now have it for lunch on a regular basis. Everyone at work wants to know how to make it.

—Michael Steffens, Indianapolis, IN

TAKES: 15 min. • **MAKES:** 1 serving

- 2 **Tbsp. hummus**
- 1 **whole wheat tortilla (8 in.)**
- ¼ **cup torn mixed salad greens**
- 2 **Tbsp. finely chopped sweet onion**
- 2 **Tbsp. thinly sliced cucumber**
- 2 **Tbsp. alfalfa sprouts**
- 2 **Tbsp. shredded carrot**
- 1 **Tbsp. balsamic vinaigrette**

Spread hummus over tortilla. Layer with salad greens, onion, cucumber, sprouts and carrot. Drizzle with vinaigrette. Roll up tightly.

1 WRAP: 235 cal., 8g fat (1g sat. fat), 0 chol., 415mg sod., 32g carb. (4g sugars, 5g fiber), 7g pro. **DIABETIC EXCHANGES:** 2 starch, 1 fat.

FAVORITE WILD RICE SOUP

I'm crazy about homemade soup during the fall and winter months. This wild rice incarnation is one of my favorite cool-weather experiments.
—Deborah Williams, Peoria, AZ

PREP: 10 min. • **COOK:** 50 min. • **MAKES:** 6 servings

- 2 cups water
- ⅓ cup uncooked wild rice
- ¾ tsp. salt, divided
- ¼ cup butter, cubed
- 1 medium onion, finely chopped
- 2 celery ribs, finely chopped
- ¼ cup all-purpose flour
- ¼ tsp. freshly ground pepper
- 5 cups 2% milk
- 1 tsp. chicken bouillon granules

1. In a small saucepan, bring water to a boil. Stir in wild rice and ¼ tsp. salt. Reduce heat; simmer, covered, until rice kernels are puffed open, 40-45 minutes.

2. In a large heavy saucepan, heat butter over medium heat; saute the onion and celery until tender, 5-7 minutes. Stir in flour, pepper and remaining salt until blended; gradually stir in milk and bouillon. Bring to a boil, stirring constantly; cook and stir until thickened, 2-3 minutes.

3. Drain rice; add to soup. Cook, uncovered, over medium heat 5 minutes, stirring occasionally.

1 CUP: 231 cal., 12g fat (7g sat. fat), 37mg chol., 604mg sod., 23g carb. (11g sugars, 1g fiber), 9g pro.

OUR TWO CENT$

Unlike long grain rice, wild rice doesn't always absorb all of the water; you may need to drain excess cooking liquid before adding it to the soup. If you have only bouillon cubes, substitute one cube for 1 tsp. bouillon granules. Stir in leftover chicken, ham or turkey for a protein boost.

PULLED PORK GRILLED CHEESE

I combined two of my family's favorite foods: pulled pork and grilled cheese sandwiches. Use store-bought pulled pork to make this recipe super fast and easy.
—Crystal Jo Bruns, Iliff, CO

TAKES: 30 min. • **MAKES:** 4 servings

1 carton (16 oz.) refrigerated fully cooked barbecued shredded pork
1 garlic clove, minced

8 slices country white bread
6 oz. sliced Manchego cheese or 8 slices Monterey Jack cheese

1 small red onion, thinly sliced
¼ cup mayonnaise

1. Heat shredded pork according to package directions. Stir in garlic. Layer four slices of bread with cheese, onion, pork mixture and remaining bread. Spread outsides of sandwiches with mayonnaise.

2. In a large nonstick skillet, toast sandwiches in batches over medium-low heat until golden brown and cheese is melted, about 2-3 minutes per side.

1 SANDWICH: 605 cal., 29g fat (13g sat. fat), 74mg chol., 1406mg sod., 53g carb. (22g sugars, 2g fiber), 29g pro.

BLACKENED PORK CAESAR SALAD

When I cook, my goal is to have enough leftovers for lunch the next day. This Caesar salad with pork has fantastic flavor even when the meat is chilled.
—Penny Hedges, Dewdney, BC

TAKES: 30 min. • **MAKES:** 2 servings

2 Tbsp. mayonnaise
1 Tbsp. olive oil
1 Tbsp. lemon juice
1 garlic clove, minced
⅛ tsp. seasoned salt
⅛ tsp. pepper

SALAD
¾ lb. pork tenderloin, cut into 1-in. cubes
1 Tbsp. blackened seasoning
1 Tbsp. canola oil

6 cups torn romaine
Salad croutons and shredded Parmesan cheese, optional

1. For dressing, in a small bowl, mix the first six ingredients until blended.

2. Toss pork with blackened seasoning. In a large skillet, heat oil over medium-high heat. Add pork; cook and stir 5-7 minutes or until tender.

3. To serve, place romaine in a large bowl; add dressing and toss to coat. Top with pork, and, if desired, croutons and cheese.

2½ CUPS: 458 cal., 31g fat (5g sat. fat), 100mg chol., 464mg sod., 8g carb. (2g sugars, 3g fiber), 36g pro.

CILANTRO SALAD DRESSING

Use this zippy dressing over greens, as a dip for raw veggies, or as a garnish for hot or cold boiled potatoes. You'll love it.
—Sara Laber, Shelburne, VT

TAKES: 10 min. • **MAKES:** about ½ cup

- ¼ cup buttermilk
- ¼ cup fat-free mayonnaise
- 3 to 6 drops hot pepper sauce
- ¼ tsp. salt
- ¼ tsp. garlic powder
- ⅛ tsp. sugar
- ½ cup fresh cilantro leaves

Place all ingredients in a blender; cover and process until blended. Refrigerate, covered, until serving.

2 TBSP.: 18 cal., 0 fat (0 sat. fat), 1mg chol., 298mg sod., 4g carb. (2g sugars, 0 fiber), 1g pro.

MY TWO CENT$

"Made this to go over taco salad and it was a hit. I have been freezing cilantro and will try this dressing with the frozen cilantro."
—PZSIRAY, TASTEOFHOME.COM

CRISPY PORK TENDERLOIN SANDWICHES

This breaded tenderloin rekindles fond memories of a sandwich shop in my Ohio hometown. Even though I no longer live there, I'm happy to say my family and I can still enjoy one of the shop's classics thanks to this recipe.
—Erin Fitch, Sherrills Ford, NC

TAKES: 25 min. • **MAKES:** 4 servings

2 Tbsp. all-purpose flour
½ tsp. salt
¼ tsp. pepper
1 large egg, lightly beaten
½ cup seasoned bread crumbs

3 Tbsp. panko (Japanese) bread crumbs
½ lb. pork tenderloin
2 Tbsp. canola oil
4 hamburger buns or kaiser rolls, split

Optional toppings: lettuce leaves, tomato and pickle slices, and mayonnaise

1. In a shallow bowl, mix flour, salt and pepper. Place egg and the combined bread crumbs in two separate shallow bowls.

2. Cut the tenderloin crosswise into four slices; pound each with a meat mallet to ¼-in. thickness. Dip in flour mixture to coat both sides; shake off the excess. Dip in egg, then in crumb mixture, patting to help adhere.

3. In a large skillet, heat oil over medium heat. Cook the pork 2-3 minutes on each side or until golden brown. Remove from pan; drain on paper towels. Serve in buns, with toppings as desired.

1 SANDWICH: 289 cal., 11g fat (2g sat. fat), 43mg chol., 506mg sod., 29g carb. (3g sugars, 1g fiber), 17g pro. **DIABETIC EXCHANGES:** 2 starch, 2 lean meat, 1½ fat.

HEALTH TIP: Keep carbs to about 10g per serving by skipping the bun and serving the pork on grilled portobello mushrooms or eggplant slices.

PEA & PEANUT SALAD

A friend gave me the recipe for this tasty salad that's perfect for any gathering or potluck. Even folks who normally push away their peas devour this by the bowlful.
—Laurinda Nelson, Phoenix, AZ

TAKES: 15 min. • **MAKES:** 4 servings

- 2½ cups frozen peas (about 10 oz.), thawed
- 1 cup dry roasted peanuts
- 1 cup chopped celery
- 6 bacon strips, cooked and crumbled
- ¼ cup chopped red onion
- ½ cup mayonnaise
- ¼ cup prepared zesty Italian salad dressing

In a large bowl, combine the first five ingredients. In a small bowl, mix the mayonnaise and salad dressing; stir into salad. Refrigerate, covered, until serving.

⅔ **CUP:** 579 cal., 48g fat (7g sat. fat), 22mg chol., 957mg sod., 23g carb. (7g sugars, 7g fiber), 17g pro.

OUR TWO CENT$
This salad is best made right before serving. The peanuts can absorb the dressing and become soggy if made too far in advance. If you like, add the peas while they're still frozen. The salad will be refreshingly cold and crisp.

CAROLINA-STYLE VINEGAR BBQ CHICKEN

I live in Georgia but I appreciate the tangy, sweet and slightly spicy taste of Carolina vinegar chicken. I make my version in the slow cooker. When you walk in the door after being gone all day, the aroma will knock you off your feet.

—Ramona Parris, Canton, GA

PREP: 10 min. • **COOK:** 4 hours • **MAKES:** 6 servings

- 2 cups water
- 1 cup white vinegar
- ¼ cup sugar
- 1 Tbsp. reduced-sodium chicken base
- 1 tsp. crushed red pepper flakes
- ¾ tsp. salt
- 1½ lbs. boneless skinless chicken breasts
- 6 whole wheat hamburger buns, split, optional

1. In a small bowl, mix the first six ingredients. Place chicken in a 3-qt. slow cooker; add vinegar mixture. Cook, covered, on low 4-5 hours or until chicken is tender.

2. Remove chicken; cool slightly. Reserve 1 cup cooking juices; discard remaining juices. Shred chicken with two forks. Return the meat and reserved cooking juices to slow cooker; heat through. If desired, serve the chicken mixture on buns.

NOTE: Look for chicken base near the broth and bouillon.

½ CUP: 134 cal., 3g fat (1g sat. fat), 63mg chol., 228mg sod., 3g carb. (3g sugars, 0 fiber), 23g pro. **DIABETIC EXCHANGES:** 3 lean meat.

SPINACH & SAUSAGE LENTIL SOUP

This soup makes regular appearances on our dinner table during the cooler months of the year. It gets a thumbs-up from all, including my young child with discriminating tastes.
—Kalyn Gensic, Ardmore, OK

PREP: 5 min. • **COOK:** 45 min. • **MAKES:** 6 servings (2 qt.)

- 1 lb. bulk spicy pork sausage
- 1 cup dried brown lentils, rinsed
- 1 can (15 oz.) cannellini beans, rinsed and drained
- 1 carton (32 oz.) reduced-sodium chicken broth
- 1 cup water
- 1 can (14½ oz.) fire-roasted diced tomatoes, undrained
- 6 cups fresh spinach (about 4 oz.)
  Crumbled goat cheese, optional

1. In a Dutch oven, cook and crumble the pork sausage over medium heat until no longer pink, 5-7 minutes; drain.

2. Stir in lentils, beans, broth and water; bring to a boil. Reduce heat; simmer, covered, until lentils are tender, about 30 minutes. Stir in tomatoes; heat through.

3. Remove from heat; stir in spinach until wilted. If desired, serve with goat cheese.

FREEZE OPTION: Freeze cooled soup in freezer containers. To use, partially thaw in refrigerator overnight. Heat through in a saucepan, stirring occasionally.

1⅓ CUPS: 390 cal., 17g fat (5g sat. fat), 41mg chol., 1242mg sod., 37g carb. (3g sugars, 8g fiber), 22g pro.

◆ **FAST FIX**

BASIL & HEIRLOOM TOMATO TOSS

I created this garden-fresh salad to showcase the heirloom tomatoes and peppers we raised to sell at the farmers market. Experiment with other types of basil like lemon, lime, licorice and cinnamon.
—Sue Gronholz, Beaver Dam, WI

TAKES: 15 min. • **MAKES:** 4 servings

- ¼ cup olive oil
- 3 Tbsp. red wine vinegar
- 2 tsp. sugar
- 1 garlic clove, minced
- ¾ tsp. salt
- ¼ tsp. ground mustard

- ¼ tsp. pepper
- 2 large heirloom tomatoes, cut into ½-in. pieces
- 1 medium sweet yellow pepper, cut into ½-in. pieces

- ½ small red onion, thinly sliced
- 1 Tbsp. chopped fresh basil

In a large bowl, whisk the first seven ingredients until blended. Add remaining ingredients; toss gently to combine.

1 CUP: 162 cal., 14g fat (2g sat. fat), 0 chol., 449mg sod., 10g carb. (5g sugars, 2g fiber), 1g pro. **DIABETIC EXCHANGES:** 3 fat, 1 vegetable.

BEAN & BACON GRIDDLE WRAPS

These wraps stuffed with salsa, bacon and cheese make an awesome hand-held meal. I use fresh pico de gallo when I can, but a jar of salsa yields delicious results, too.
—Stacy Mullens, Gresham, OR

TAKES: 20 min. • **MAKES:** 4 servings

- 1 can (16 oz.) fat-free refried beans
- ½ cup salsa, divided
- 4 flour tortillas (8 in.)
- ½ cup crumbled cotija cheese or shredded Monterey Jack cheese
- 3 bacon strips, cooked and coarsely chopped
- 2 cups shredded lettuce

1. In a small bowl, mix beans and ¼ cup salsa until blended. Place tortillas on a griddle; cook over medium heat 1 minute, then turn over. Place the bean mixture, cheese and bacon onto centers of tortillas; cook 1-2 minutes longer or until tortillas begin to crisp.

2. Remove from griddle; immediately top with lettuce and remaining salsa. To serve, fold the bottom and sides of tortilla over filling.

HEALTH TIP: Use Amy's Organic Light in Sodium Refried Beans or Eden Food Lightly Salted Refried Beans and save almost 300 mg sodium per serving.

1 WRAP: 375 cal., 10g fat (4g sat. fat), 21mg chol., 1133mg sod., 52g carb. (1g sugars, 8g fiber), 18g pro.

EASY WHITE CHICKEN CHILI

Chili is one of our best strategies for warming up in cold weather. We use chicken and white beans for a twist on the regular bowl of red. It's soothing comfort food.
—Rachel Lewis, Danville, VA

TAKES: 30 min. • **MAKES:** 6 servings

1 lb. lean ground chicken
1 medium onion, chopped
2 cans (15 oz. each) cannellini beans, rinsed and drained
1 can (4 oz.) chopped green chilies

1 tsp. ground cumin
½ tsp. dried oregano
¼ tsp. pepper
1 can (14½ oz.) reduced-sodium chicken broth

Optional toppings: reduced-fat sour cream, shredded cheddar cheese and chopped fresh cilantro

1. In a large saucepan, cook chicken and onion over medium-high heat 6-8 minutes or until chicken is no longer pink, breaking up chicken into crumbles.

2. Place one can of beans in a small bowl; mash slightly. Stir mashed beans, remaining can of beans, chilies, seasonings and broth into chicken mixture; bring to a boil. Reduce heat; simmer, covered, 12-15 minutes or until the flavors are blended. Serve with toppings as desired.

FREEZE OPTION: Freeze cooled chili in freezer containers. To use, partially thaw in refrigerator overnight. Heat through in a saucepan, stirring occasionally and adding a little broth if necessary.

1 CUP: 228 cal., 5g fat (1g sat. fat), 54mg chol., 504mg sod., 23g carb. (1g sugars, 6g fiber), 22g pro. **DIABETIC EXCHANGES:** 3 lean meat, 1½ starch.

TANGY PULLED PORK SANDWICHES

The magic of the slow cooker is not limited to making easy meals. In this recipe, it also keeps the pork tender, saucy and loaded with flavor.
—Beki Kosydar-Krantz, Mayfield, PA

PREP: 10 min. • **COOK:** 4 hours • **MAKES:** 4 servings

- 1 pork tenderloin (1 lb.)
- 1 cup ketchup
- 2 Tbsp. plus 1½ tsp. brown sugar
- 2 Tbsp. plus 1½ tsp. cider vinegar
- 1 Tbsp. plus 1½ tsp. Worcestershire sauce
- 1 Tbsp. spicy brown mustard
- ¼ tsp. pepper
- 4 rolls or buns, split and toasted
  Coleslaw, optional

1. Cut the tenderloin in half; place in a 3-qt. slow cooker. Combine the ketchup, brown sugar, vinegar, Worcestershire sauce, mustard and pepper; pour over pork.

2. Cover and cook on low for 4-5 hours or until meat is tender. Remove meat; shred with two forks. Return to slow cooker; heat through. Serve on toasted rolls or buns, and, if desired, with coleslaw.

1 SANDWICH: 402 cal., 7g fat (2g sat. fat), 63mg chol., 1181mg sod., 56g carb. (18g sugars, 2g fiber), 29g pro. **DIABETIC EXCHANGES:** 3½ starch, 3 lean meat, 1 fat.

ECONOMICAL ODDS & ENDS

Whether you're looking for a tasty hot bite or special sauce to include with dinner, a sweet bread or jam to share with a neighbor, or simply want something to nibble when hunger strikes, look here for the best mix of munchies, snacks and other wallet-friendly options.

ONE-BOWL CHOCOLATE CHIP BREAD

My family of chocoholics hops out of bed on Valentine's Day because they know I'm baking this indulgent quick bread for breakfast. But don't wait for a special occasion to enjoy it. It hits the spot any time of year.
—Angela Lively, Conroe, TX

PREP: 20 min. • **BAKE:** 65 minutes • **MAKES:** 1 loaf (16 slices)

3 large eggs
1 cup sugar

2 cups sour cream
3 cups self-rising flour

2 cups (12 oz.) semisweet chocolate chips

1. Preheat oven to 350°. Beat eggs, sugar and sour cream until well blended. Gradually stir in flour. Fold in chocolate chips. Transfer to a greased 9x5-in. loaf pan.

2. Bake until a toothpick comes out clean, 65-75 minutes. Cool in pan 5 minutes before removing to a wire rack to cool.

NOTE: As a substitute for 3 cups of self-rising flour, place 4½ tsp. baking powder and 1½ tsp. salt in a 1-cup measuring cup. Add enough all-purpose flour to measure 1 cup; combine with an additional 2 cups all-purpose flour.

1 SLICE: 306 cal., 13g fat (8g sat. fat), 42mg chol., 305mg sod., 44g carb. (25g sugars, 2g fiber), 5g pro.

BARBECUE CHICKEN TOSTADAS

Lots of my recipes start out as fun ways to use leftovers—like this one! My kids love tostadas, so this day-after-cookout dinner was a big hit.
—Lauren Wyler, Dripping Springs, TX

TAKES: 30 min. • **MAKES:** 4 servings

- 2 Tbsp. lemon juice
- 2 Tbsp. mayonnaise
- 1 Tbsp. light brown sugar
- ⅛ tsp. pepper
- 2 cups coleslaw mix
- 2 green onions, thinly sliced
- 1 cup baked beans
- 2⅔ cups shredded cooked chicken
- ⅔ cup barbecue sauce
- 8 tostada shells
- 1 cup shredded smoked cheddar cheese

1. Preheat broiler. Mix first four ingredients; toss with coleslaw mix and green onions. Refrigerate until serving.

2. Place baked beans in a small saucepan; mash with a potato masher until smooth. Cook over low heat until heated through, about 10 minutes, stirring frequently.

3. In another saucepan, mix the chicken and barbecue sauce; cook over medium-low heat until heated through, about 10 minutes, stirring occasionally.

4. To assemble, place the tostada shells on ungreased baking sheets. Spread with beans; top with the chicken mixture and cheese. Broil 3-4 in. from heat until tostada shells are lightly browned and cheese is melted, 1-2 minutes. Top with slaw. Serve immediately.

2 TOSTADAS: 612 cal., 29g fat (10g sat. fat), 116mg chol., 1113mg sod., 51g carb. (21g sugars, 6g fiber), 39g pro.

EVERYTHING BAGEL CHICKEN STRIPS

I love the flavor profile of everything bagels and decided to use it for a different take on breaded chicken fingers. Serve them with your favorite chicken finger dip.
—Cyndy Gerken, Naples, FL

TAKES: 30 min. • **MAKES:** 4 servings

- 1 day-old everything bagel, torn
- ½ cup panko (Japanese) bread crumbs
- ½ cup grated Parmesan cheese
- ¼ tsp. crushed red pepper flakes
- ¼ cup butter, cubed
- 1 lb. chicken tenderloins
- ½ tsp. salt

1. Preheat oven to 425°. Pulse the torn bagel in a food processor until coarse crumbs form. Place ½ cup bagel crumbs in a shallow bowl; toss with panko, cheese and pepper flakes. (Save the remaining bagel crumbs for another use.)

2. In a microwave-safe shallow bowl, microwave butter until melted. Sprinkle the chicken with salt. Dip in warm butter, then coat with crumb mixture, patting to help adhere. Place strips on a greased rack in a 15x10x1-in. pan.

3. Bake until golden brown and chicken is no longer pink, 15-17 minutes.

1 SERVING: 246 cal., 12g fat (7g sat. fat), 85mg chol., 593mg sod., 6g carb. (0 sugars, 0 fiber), 30g pro.

OUR TWO CENT$

One bagel will yield about 2 cups crumbs. Save the leftover crumbs to make a tasty topping for a casserole or use as a binding agent in meat loaves and meatballs. For more flavor and impact, add dried minced onion and/or garlic powder to the crumb mixture.

GINGER PEAR FREEZER JAM

At dinner with friends one evening, the lady of the house served us some pears she had preserved with ginger and lemon. The flavor was heavenly. When she gave us fresh pears, I decided to try my hand at making a ginger and lemon freezer jam.

—Jeni Pittard, Statham, GA

PREP: 30 min. • **COOK:** 10 min. + standing • **MAKES:** 7 cups

5½ cups finely chopped peeled fresh pears (about 10 medium)
1 pkg. (1¾ oz.) pectin for lower sugar recipes

2 Tbsp. lemon juice
1½ tsp. grated lemon zest
1 tsp. minced fresh gingerroot

4 cups sugar
1 tsp. vanilla extract

1. Rinse seven 1-cup plastic containers and lids with boiling water. Dry thoroughly. In a Dutch oven, combine pears, pectin, lemon juice, lemon zest and ginger. Bring to a full rolling boil over high heat, stirring constantly. Stir in sugar. Boil for 1 minute, stirring constantly. Stir in vanilla.

2. Remove from heat; skim off foam. Immediately fill all containers to within ½ in. of tops. Wipe off top edges of containers; immediately cover with lids. Let stand at room temperature 24 hours.

3. Jam is now ready to use. Refrigerate up to 3 weeks or freeze extra containers up to 12 months. Thaw frozen jam in refrigerator before serving.

2 TBSP.: 64 cal., 0 fat (0 sat. fat), 0 chol., 9mg sod., 17g carb. (16g sugars, 0 fiber), 0 pro.

PEPPERONI PIZZA BAKED POTATOES

These tasty taters were a spur-of-the-moment recipe I created from leftovers. It's a mash-up that combines two dinnertime favorites into one super fun meal.
—Dawn Lowenstein, Huntingdon Valley, PA

TAKES: 30 min. • **MAKES:** 4 servings

- 4 medium russet potatoes (about 8 oz. each)
- 1 Tbsp. olive oil
- 1 cup sliced fresh mushrooms
- 1 small green pepper, chopped
- 1 small onion, chopped
- 1 garlic clove, minced
- 1 can (8 oz.) pizza sauce
- ⅓ cup mini sliced turkey pepperoni
- ½ cup shredded Italian cheese blend
- Fresh oregano leaves or dried oregano, optional

1. Preheat oven to 400°. Scrub potatoes; place on a microwave-safe plate. Pierce several times with a fork. Microwave, uncovered, on high until tender, 12-15 minutes.

2. In a large skillet, heat oil over medium-high heat; saute mushrooms, pepper and onion until tender, 6-8 minutes. Add the garlic; cook and stir 1 minute. Stir in the pizza sauce and pepperoni; heat through.

3. Place potatoes on a baking sheet; cut an X in the top of each. Fluff pulp with a fork. Top with vegetable mixture; sprinkle with cheese. Bake until cheese is melted, 5-7 minutes. If desired, sprinkle with oregano.

1 BAKED POTATO WITH TOPPINGS: 311 cal., 9g fat (3g sat. fat), 23mg chol., 515mg sod., 46g carb. (5g sugars, 6g fiber), 13g pro. **DIABETIC EXCHANGES:** 3 starch, 1 medium-fat meat, ½ fat.

REFRIGERATOR JALAPENO DILL PICKLES

I'm passionate about making pickles. My husband is passionate about eating them. He's too impatient to let them cure on the shelf, so I found this quick recipe to make him happy. Add hotter peppers if you like.
—Annie Jensen, Roseau, MN

PREP: 20 min. + chilling • **MAKES:** about 4 dozen pickle spears

3 lbs. pickling cucumbers (about 12)	¼ cup snipped fresh dill	2½ cups water
1 small onion, halved and sliced	1 to 2 jalapeno peppers, sliced	2½ cups cider vinegar
	3 garlic cloves, minced	⅓ cup canning salt
		⅓ cup sugar

1. Cut each cucumber lengthwise into four spears. In an extra-large bowl, combine the cucumbers, onion, dill, jalapenos and garlic. In a large saucepan, combine water, vinegar, salt and sugar. Bring to a boil; cook and stir just until salt and sugar are dissolved. Pour over cucumber mixture; cool.

2. Cover tightly and refrigerate for at least 24 hours. Store in the refrigerator for up to 2 months.

NOTE: Wear disposable gloves when cutting hot peppers; the oils can burn skin. Avoid touching your face.

1 PICKLE: 4 cal., 0 fat (0 sat. fat), 0 chol., 222mg sod., 1g carb. (0 sugars, 0 fiber), 0 pro.

MY TWO CENT$

"These were fantastic and so easy to make! I used dried dill weed in place of fresh."
—ANGEL182009, TASTEOFHOME.COM

SICILIAN MEAT SAUCE

People have told me this sauce is better than the gravy their Sicilian grandmothers used to make. But don't tell the old generation that! Serve the sauce with your favorite cooked pasta.
—Emory Doty, Jasper, GA

PREP: 30 min. • **COOK:** 6 hours • **MAKES:** 12 servings

- 3 Tbsp. olive oil, divided
- 3 lbs. bone-in country-style pork ribs
- 1 medium onion, chopped
- 3 to 5 garlic cloves, minced
- 2 cans (28 oz. each) crushed or diced tomatoes, drained
- 1 can (14½ oz.) Italian diced tomatoes, drained
- 3 bay leaves

- 2 Tbsp. chopped fresh parsley
- 2 Tbsp. chopped capers, drained
- ½ tsp. dried basil
- ½ tsp. dried rosemary, crushed
- ½ tsp. dried thyme
- ½ tsp. crushed red pepper flakes

- ½ tsp. salt
- ½ tsp. sugar
- 1 cup beef broth
- ½ cup dry red wine or additional beef broth
  Hot cooked pasta
  Grated Parmesan cheese, optional

1. In a Dutch oven, heat 2 Tbsp. olive oil over medium-high heat. Brown pork ribs in batches; transfer to a 6-qt. slow cooker.

2. Add remaining oil to Dutch oven; saute onion for 2 minutes. Add garlic; cook 1 minute more. Add next 11 ingredients. Pour in broth and red wine; bring to a light boil. Transfer to the slow cooker. Cook, covered, until the pork is tender, about 6 hours.

3. Discard bay leaves. Remove meat from slow cooker; shred or pull apart, discarding bones. Return meat to the sauce. Serve over pasta; if desired, sprinkle with Parmesan cheese.

1 CUP: 214 cal., 11g fat (3g sat. fat), 44mg chol., 822mg sod., 13g carb. (8g sugars, 3g fiber), 16g pro.

BUFFALO CHICKEN BISCUITS

Muffin tin recipes make fantastic finger food. These spicy, savory muffins are always a hit at parties. We love them as a simple snack on game day, too.
—Jasmin Baron, Livonia, NY

PREP: 20 min. • **BAKE:** 25 min. • **MAKES:** 1 dozen

- 3 cups chopped rotisserie chicken
- ¼ cup Louisiana-style hot sauce
- 2 cups biscuit/baking mix
- ¼ tsp. celery seed
- ⅛ tsp. pepper

- 1 large egg
- ½ cup 2% milk
- ¼ cup ranch salad dressing
- 1½ cups shredded Colby-Monterey Jack cheese, divided

- 2 green onions, thinly sliced
  Additional ranch dressing and hot sauce, optional

1. Preheat oven to 400°. Toss chicken with hot sauce. In large bowl, whisk together baking mix, celery seed and pepper. In another bowl, whisk together egg, milk and dressing; add to the dry ingredients, stirring just until moistened. Fold in 1 cup cheese, green onions and chicken mixture.

2. Spoon into 12 greased muffin cups. Sprinkle with remaining cheese. Bake until a toothpick inserted in the center comes out clean, about 25-30 minutes.

3. Cool 5 minutes before removing from pan to a wire rack. Serve warm. If desired, serve with additional dressing and hot sauce. Refrigerate leftover biscuits.

2 BISCUITS: 461 cal., 24g fat (10g sat. fat), 121mg chol., 1180mg sod., 29g carb. (3g sugars, 1g fiber), 31g pro.

EGGPLANT FLATBREAD PIZZAS

I'm a professional chef and love to make a variety of different foods. I've been making these flatbread pizzas long before my chef days. They were a favorite then and remain a favorite now.
—Christine Wendland, Browns Mills, NJ

TAKES: 30 min. • **MAKES:** 4 servings

- 3 Tbsp. olive oil, divided
- 2½ cups cubed eggplant (½ in.)
- 1 small onion, halved and thinly sliced
- ½ tsp. salt
- ⅛ tsp. pepper
- 1 garlic clove, minced
- 2 naan flatbreads
- ½ cup part-skim ricotta cheese
- 1 tsp. dried oregano
- ½ cup roasted garlic tomato sauce
- ½ cup loosely packed basil leaves
- 1 cup shredded part-skim mozzarella cheese
- 2 Tbsp. grated Parmesan cheese
  Sliced fresh basil, optional

1. Preheat oven to 400°. In a large skillet, heat 1 Tbsp. oil over medium-high heat; saute the eggplant and onion with salt and pepper until eggplant begins to soften, 4-5 minutes. Stir in garlic; remove from heat.

2. Place naan flatbreads on a baking sheet. Spread with ricotta cheese; sprinkle with the oregano. Spread with tomato sauce. Top with eggplant mixture and whole basil leaves. Sprinkle with mozzarella and Parmesan cheeses; drizzle with remaining oil.

3. Bake until crust is golden brown and cheese is melted, 12-15 minutes. If desired, top pizzas with sliced basil.

NOTE: Roasted garlic tomato sauce may be substituted with any flavored tomato sauce or a meatless pasta sauce.

½ PIZZA: 340 cal., 21g fat (7g sat. fat), 32mg chol., 996mg sod., 25g carb. (5g sugars, 3g fiber), 14g pro.

QUINOA UNSTUFFED PEPPERS

This deconstructed stuffed pepper dish packs a wallop of flavor. I make this one again and again, and I make sure my freezer's stocked with single-serve portions to take to work.
—Rebecca Ende, Phoenix, NY

TAKES: 30 min. • **MAKES:** 4 servings

- 1½ cups vegetable stock
- ¾ cup quinoa, rinsed
- 1 lb. Italian turkey sausage links, casings removed
- 1 medium sweet red pepper, chopped
- 1 medium green pepper, chopped
- ¾ cup chopped sweet onion
- 1 garlic clove, minced
- ¼ tsp. garam masala
- ¼ tsp. pepper
- ⅛ tsp. salt

1. In a small saucepan, bring stock to a boil. Add quinoa. Reduce heat; simmer, covered, until the liquid is absorbed, 12-15 minutes. Remove from the heat.

2. In a large skillet, cook and crumble sausage with peppers and onion over medium-high heat until no longer pink, 8-10 minutes. Add garlic and seasonings; cook and stir 1 minute. Stir in quinoa.

FREEZE OPTION: Place cooled quinoa mixture in freezer containers. To use, partially thaw in the refrigerator overnight. Microwave, covered, on high in a microwave-safe dish until the mixture is heated through, stirring occasionally.

1 CUP: 261 cal., 9g fat (2g sat. fat), 42mg chol., 760mg sod., 28g carb. (3g sugars, 4g fiber), 17g pro. **DIABETIC EXCHANGES:** 2 starch, 2 medium-fat meat.

OUR TWO CENT$
If you don't have vegetable stock on hand, feel free to use chicken or beef stock. Broth can be used, too, but remember that broth is already seasoned. Think of stock like a blank canvas where you can layer on ingredients and seasonings for a fusion of unique flavors.

POTATO-SAUSAGE FOIL PACKS

We had these smoky campfire bundles at a friend's house for dinner and loved the simplicity of this great outdoor meal. Now we regularly make it for weeknight dinners when the weather is in our favor.
—Alissa Keith, Forest, VA

PREP: 20 min. • **GRILL:** 30 min. • **MAKES:** 4 servings

- 1 medium green pepper
- 1 medium sweet red pepper
- 1 medium sweet yellow pepper
- 1 pkg. (14 oz.) smoked turkey kielbasa, sliced
- 2 large potatoes, cut into wedges
- 1 medium onion, chopped
- 4 tsp. lemon juice
- 4 tsp. olive oil
- ½ tsp. garlic powder
- ½ tsp. pepper
  Lemon wedges, optional

1. Cut peppers into 1-in. pieces; place in a large bowl. Toss with remaining ingredients. Divide the mixture among four double thicknesses of heavy-duty foil (about 18x12 in.). Fold the foil around mixture, sealing tightly.

2. Grill, covered, over medium heat until potatoes are tender, 30-35 minutes. Open foil carefully to allow steam to escape. If desired, serve packets with lemon wedges.

1 SERVING: 344 cal., 10g fat (2g sat. fat), 62mg chol., 990mg sod., 42g carb. (8g sugars, 6g fiber), 21g pro.

SWEETS ON THE CHEAP

Dessert doesn't have to cost a fortune.
Enjoy these budget-friendly sweet treats sure
to bring big smiles to all who taste them.

CEREAL & MILK ICE CREAM SANDWICHES

It's OK, go ahead and buy those forbidden sweetened breakfast cereals you normally pass by. You—and the kids—will be glad you did when you try these fun ice cream sandwiches.
—*Taste of Home* Test Kitchen

PREP: 10 min. + freezing • **MAKES:** 4 servings

- 2 Tbsp. Cap'n Crunch cereal
- 2 Tbsp. Froot Loops cereal
- 2 Tbsp. Fruity Pebbles cereal
- ¾ cup dulce de leche ice cream, softened
- 4 Rice Krispies treats (2.2 oz. each), halved lengthwise
- 1 Tbsp. hot caramel ice cream topping, warmed

In a shallow bowl, combine cereals. Spread ice cream onto the bottom half of each Rice Krispies treat. Drizzle with ice cream topping. Replace top half of Rice Krispies treat. Roll sides in the cereal mixture. Place on a baking sheet; freeze for at least 1 hour.

1 ICE CREAM SANDWICH: 381 cal., 9g fat (4g sat. fat), 38mg chol., 427mg sod., 70g carb. (30g sugars, 0 fiber), 5g pro.

APPLE DUMPLING BAKE

I received this recipe from a friend, then tweaked it a bit for my family. Mountain Dew is the secret ingredient in this rich apple dessert that tastes as good as it looks.
—Chris Shields, Monrovia, IN

PREP: 15 min. • **BAKE:** 35 min. • **MAKES:** 8 servings

- 2 medium Granny Smith apples
- 2 tubes (8 oz. each) refrigerated crescent rolls
- 1 cup sugar
- ⅓ cup butter, softened
- ½ tsp. ground cinnamon
- ¾ cup Mountain Dew soda
- Vanilla ice cream

1. Preheat oven to 350°. Peel, core and cut each apple into eight wedges. Unroll both tubes of the crescent dough; separate each into eight triangles. Wrap a triangle around each apple wedge. Place in a greased 13x9-in. baking dish.

2. In a bowl, mix sugar, butter and cinnamon until blended; sprinkle over dumplings. Slowly pour soda around the rolls (do not stir).

3. Bake, uncovered, until golden brown and apples are tender, 35-40 minutes. Serve warm with ice cream.

2 DUMPLINGS: 414 cal., 20g fat (9g sat. fat), 20mg chol., 510mg sod., 55g carb. (35g sugars, 1g fiber), 4g pro.

LEMON MERINGUE FLOATS

The idea for this ice cream float came to me in a dream. When I woke up, I knew I had to make it. Thank you, Mr. Sandman!
—Cindy Reams, Philipsburg, PA

TAKES: 5 min. • **MAKES:** 6 servings

- 3 **cups vanilla ice cream,**
  softened if necessary
- 18 **miniature meringue**
  cookies
- 6 **cups cold pink lemonade**

Place ½ cup ice cream and three cookies in each of six tall glasses. Top with lemonade. Serve immediately.

1½ CUPS WITH 3 COOKIES: 282 cal., 7g fat (4g sat. fat), 29mg chol., 77mg sod., 51g carb. (48g sugars, 0 fiber), 3g pro.

HEALTH TIP: Make your floats with frozen yogurt for a slimmed-down treat.

OUR TWO CENT$
Ice cream floats can be an easy and fun dessert for a summer shindig. Take them over the top with rainbow sprinkles or other edible decorations.

S'MORES CRESCENT ROLLS

Here's how to score indoor s'mores: Grab crescent dough and Nutella. Invite the kids to help with this rolled-up version of the campfire classic.
—Cathy Trochelman, Brookfield, WI

TAKES: 25 min. • **MAKES:** 8 servings

- 1 tube (8 oz.) refrigerated crescent rolls
- ¼ cup Nutella, divided
- 2 whole graham crackers, broken up
- 2 Tbsp. milk chocolate chips
- ⅔ cup miniature marshmallows

1. Preheat oven to 375°. Unroll crescent dough and separate into eight triangles. Place 1 tsp. Nutella at the wide end of each triangle; sprinkle with the graham crackers, chocolate chips and marshmallows. Roll up and place on ungreased baking sheets, point side down; curve to form crescents. Bake 9-11 minutes or until rolls are golden brown.

2. In a microwave, warm remaining Nutella to reach a drizzling consistency; spoon over rolls. Serve warm.

1 ROLL: 201 cal., 10g fat (3g sat. fat), 1mg chol., 256mg sod., 25g carb. (12g sugars, 1g fiber), 3g pro.

FIRST-PLACE COCONUT MACAROONS

These cookies earned a first-place ribbon at the county fair. They remain my husband's favorite cookie—whenever I make them to give away, he asks me where his batch is. I especially like the fact that the recipe makes a not-too-big batch for the two of us to nibble on.
—Penny Ann Habeck, Shawano, WI

PREP: 10 min. • **BAKE:** 20 min. + cooling • **MAKES:** about 1½ dozen

1⅓ cups sweetened
    shredded coconut

⅓ cup sugar
2 Tbsp. all-purpose flour
⅛ tsp. salt

2 large egg whites
½ tsp. vanilla extract

1. In a small bowl, combine the coconut, sugar, flour and salt. Add the egg whites and vanilla; mix well.

2. Drop by rounded teaspoonfuls onto greased baking sheets. Bake at 325° for 18-20 minutes or until golden brown. Cool on a wire rack.

1 COOKIE: 54 cal., 2g fat (2g sat. fat), 0 chol., 41mg sod., 8g carb. (7g sugars, 0 fiber), 1g pro. **DIABETIC EXCHANGES:** ½ starch, ½ fat.

MY TWO CENT$

"Crispy little bites of deliciousness!"
—SAEMMETT, TASTEOFHOME.COM

▶ **5 INGREDIENTS**

FROZEN BERRY & YOGURT SWIRLS

I enjoy these frozen yogurt pops because they double as a healthy snack and a cool, creamy sweet treat. Try them with clementines for a citrusy twist.
—Colleen Ludovice, Wauwatosa, WI

PREP: 15 min. + freezing • **MAKES:** 10 pops

10 plastic or paper cups (3 oz. each)	1 cup mixed fresh berries	2 Tbsp. sugar
2¾ cups fat-free honey Greek yogurt	¼ cup water	10 wooden pop sticks

1. Fill each cup with about ¼ cup yogurt. Place berries, water and sugar in a food processor; pulse until berries are finely chopped. Spoon 1½ Tbsp. berry mixture into each cup. Stir gently with a pop stick to swirl.

2. Top cups with foil; insert pop sticks through foil. Freeze until firm.

1 POP: 60 cal., 0 fat (0 sat. fat), 0 chol., 28mg sod., 9g carb. (8g sugars, 1g fiber), 6g pro. **DIABETIC EXCHANGES:** 1 starch.

OUR TWO CENT$
To make frozen Clementine & Yogurt Swirls, substitute 1 cup seeded clementine segments (about 5 medium) and ¼ cup orange juice for berries, water and sugar; proceed as directed.

ROOT BEER FLOAT PIE

This is one of those recipes your kids will always remember. You'll remember how easy it is to make. The only appliance you need is your freezer.
—Cindy Reams, Philipsburg, PA

PREP: 15 min. + chilling • **MAKES:** 8 servings

- 1 carton (8 oz.) frozen reduced-fat whipped topping, thawed, divided
- ¾ cup cold diet root beer
- ½ cup fat-free milk
- 1 pkg. (1 oz.) sugar-free instant vanilla pudding mix
- 1 graham cracker crust (9 in.)
  Maraschino cherries, optional

1. Set aside and refrigerate ½ cup whipped topping for garnish. In a large bowl, whisk the root beer, milk and pudding mix for 2 minutes. Fold in half of the remaining whipped topping. Spread into graham cracker crust.

2. Spread remaining whipped topping over pie. Freeze for at least 8 hours or overnight.

3. Dollop reserved whipped topping over each serving; top with a maraschino cherry if desired.

1 PIECE: 185 cal., 8g fat (4g sat. fat), 0 chol., 275mg sod., 27g carb. (14g sugars, 0 fiber), 1g pro. **DIABETIC EXCHANGES:** 2 starch, 1 fat.

PRETZEL GELATIN DESSERT

This is one of my mother's all-time favorite desserts. The salty pretzel crust is the perfect complement to the sweet cream cheese filling.
—Erin Frakes, Moline, IL

PREP: 30 min. + chilling • **MAKES:** 12 servings

2 cups crushed pretzels
¾ cup butter, melted
2 Tbsp. sugar

FILLING

1 pkg. (8 oz.) cream cheese, softened

1 cup sugar
1 carton (8 oz.) frozen whipped topping, thawed

TOPPING

2 pkg. (3 oz. each) strawberry gelatin

2 cups boiling water
½ cup cold water
Fresh strawberries and additional whipped topping, optional

1. Preheat oven to 350°. Mix crushed pretzels, melted butter and sugar; press onto bottom of an ungreased 13x9-in. baking dish. Bake for 10 minutes. Cool completely.

2. For filling, beat cream cheese and sugar until smooth. Stir in whipped topping; spread over crust. Refrigerate, covered, until cold.

3. In a small bowl, dissolve gelatin in boiling water. Stir in cold water; refrigerate until partially set. Pour carefully over filling. Refrigerate, covered, until firm, 4-6 hours.

4. Cut into squares. If desired, serve with strawberries and additional whipped topping.

1 PIECE: 401 cal., 22g fat (14g sat. fat), 50mg chol., 401mg sod., 48g carb. (37g sugars, 1g fiber), 4g pro.

SNICKERDOODLES

The history of these whimsically named treats is widely disputed, but their popularity is undeniable! Help yourself to one of our soft cinnamon-sugared cookies and see for yourself.
—*Taste of Home* Test Kitchen

PREP: 20 min. • **BAKE:** 10 min./batch • **MAKES:** 2½ dozen

½ cup butter, softened
1 cup plus 2 Tbsp. sugar, divided

1 large egg
½ tsp. vanilla extract
1½ cups all-purpose flour

¼ tsp. baking soda
¼ tsp. cream of tartar
1 tsp. ground cinnamon

1. Preheat oven to 375°. Cream the butter and 1 cup sugar until light and fluffy; beat in egg and vanilla. In another bowl, whisk together flour, baking soda and cream of tartar; gradually beat into creamed mixture.

2. In a small bowl, mix cinnamon and remaining sugar. Shape dough into 1-in. balls; roll in the cinnamon sugar. Place 2 in. apart on ungreased baking sheets.

3. Bake until light brown, 10-12 minutes. Remove from pans to wire racks to cool.

1 COOKIE: 81 cal., 3g fat (2g sat. fat), 15mg chol., 44mg sod., 12g carb. (7g sugars, 0 fiber), 1g pro.

PEACH COBBLER DUMP CAKE

This recipe gives you the best of both worlds—sweet, tender cake with a beautifully crisp and buttery almond topping. Add a scoop of vanilla ice cream on the side, and dessert's golden.
—Keri Sparks, Little Elm, TX

PREP: 10 min. • **BAKE:** 35 min. • **MAKES:** 15 servings

- 2 cans (15 oz. each) sliced peaches in extra-light syrup
- 2 Tbsp. brown sugar
- 1 tsp. ground cinnamon
- 1 pkg. yellow cake mix (regular size)
- ¾ cup sliced almonds
- ½ cup cold butter

1. Preheat the oven to 350°. Place one can of peaches in a greased 13x9-in. baking dish. Drain remaining can of peaches and add to the baking dish; sprinkle with brown sugar and cinnamon. Sprinkle with cake mix and almonds.

2. Cut butter into very thin slices; arrange over top, spacing evenly. Bake until golden brown and fruit is bubbly, 35-40 minutes. Serve warm.

1 SERVING: 234 cal., 11g fat (5g sat. fat), 16mg chol., 242mg sod., 34g carb. (22g sugars, 1g fiber), 2g pro.

MY TWO CENT$

"This was extremely quick and easy to assemble. It's inexpensive to make. The house smelled delicious as it baked. The only change I made was using pecans instead of almonds to avoid a trip to the store. We will definitely make this again."
—LORRI, TASTEOFHOME.COM

RHUBARB MALLOW COBBLER

My mom used to make this when I was growing up. These days we take fresh rhubarb to my son in Texas so he can share this treat with his family.
—Judy Kay Warwick, Webster City, IA

PREP: 15 min. • **BAKE:** 40 min. • **MAKES:** 12 servings

- 4 cups diced fresh or frozen rhubarb
- 2½ cups sugar, divided
- 1 cup miniature marshmallows
- ½ cup butter, softened
- 1 tsp. vanilla extract
- 1¾ cups all-purpose flour
- 3 tsp. baking powder
- ½ tsp. salt
- ½ cup whole milk

1. In a large bowl, combine rhubarb and 1½ cups sugar. Transfer to a greased 11x7-in. baking dish. Sprinkle with marshmallows.

2. In a small bowl, cream the butter, vanilla and remaining sugar until light and fluffy. Combine the flour, baking powder and salt; add to the creamed mixture alternately with milk. Beat just until moistened; spoon over rhubarb.

3. Bake at 350° for 40-45 minutes or until the topping is golden brown. Serve warm.

NOTE: If using frozen rhubarb, measure rhubarb while still frozen, then thaw completely. Drain in a colander, but do not press liquid out.

1 SERVING: 323 cal., 8g fat (5g sat. fat), 22mg chol., 285mg sod., 61g carb. (45g sugars, 1g fiber), 3g pro.

CINNAMON PECAN BARS

I'm a special education teacher, and we bake these tasty bars in my life skills class. It's an easy recipe my students have fun preparing. If you can't find butter pecan cake mix, yellow cake mix achieves equally delicious results.

—Jennifer Peters, Adams Center, NY

PREP: 10 min. • **BAKE:** 25 min. • **MAKES:** 2 dozen

- 1 pkg. butter pecan cake mix (regular size)
- ½ cup packed dark brown sugar
- 2 large eggs
- ½ cup butter, melted
- ½ cup chopped pecans
- ½ cup cinnamon baking chips

1. Preheat oven to 350°. In a large bowl, combine cake mix and brown sugar. Add eggs and melted butter; mix well. Stir in pecans and baking chips. Spread into a greased 13x9-in. baking pan.

2. Bake until golden brown, 25-30 minutes. Cool in pan on a wire rack. Cut into bars.

1 BAR: 185 cal., 9g fat (4g sat. fat), 26mg chol., 190mg sod., 25g carb. (17g sugars, 0 fiber), 2g pro. **DIABETIC EXCHANGES:** 1½ starch, 1½ fat.

MY TWO CENT$

"These bars are wonderful. I followed the recipe exactly. Everyone at the event I took them to asked who made them and if they could have the recipe. Many asked if there were any leftovers for them to take home. I will keep this on my list of favorites."

—FMMSLKL, TASTEOFHOME.COM

CARAMEL APPLE CUPCAKES

Bring these extra-special cupcakes to your next event and watch how quickly they disappear. With a gooey caramel topping and a spice cake base, they're the perfect mix of two fall favorites.
—Diane Halferty, Corpus Christi, TX

PREP: 25 min. • **BAKE:** 20 min. + cooling • **MAKES:** 1 dozen

1 pkg. spice or carrot cake mix (regular size)

2 cups chopped peeled tart apples (about 2 medium)
20 caramels
3 Tbsp. 2% milk

1 cup finely chopped pecans, toasted
12 wooden skewers (4½ in.)

1. Preheat oven to 350°. Line 12 jumbo muffin cups with paper liners.

2. Prepare cake mix batter according to package directions; fold in apples. Fill the prepared cups three-fourths full. Bake until a toothpick inserted in center comes out clean, about 20 minutes. Cool 10 minutes before removing from pans; cool completely on a wire rack.

3. In a small saucepan, cook caramels and milk over low heat until smooth, stirring constantly. Spread over cupcakes. Sprinkle with pecans. Insert a wooden skewer in each.

NOTE: To toast nuts, bake in a shallow pan in a 350° oven for 5-10 minutes or cook in a skillet over low heat until lightly browned, stirring occasionally.

1 CUPCAKE: 365 cal., 19g fat (3g sat. fat), 48mg chol., 315mg sod., 48g carb. (30g sugars, 1g fiber), 5g pro.